Camille 1944
If you are a bird, do not forget how to fly

Also by Claude Beccai
―――――――――――
The Cat Did It. (2012)

Claude Beccai

Camille 1944

If you are a bird, do not forget how to fly

Copyright © 2016 by Claude Beccai
First Edition November 2016
Interior pages design by Jackie Chambers
Illustrated by Jackie Chambers
Assistant Illustrator Naomi Sherk

Photo credits:
Page 58: ©Klaus D. Peter/ Wikimedia Commons/ CC-BY-SA-3.0 (2011, October, 2). *Carbide lamp* [digital image].
Retrieved from:
https://commons.m.wikimedia.org/wiki/File:Carbide_lamp.jpg
Page 99: ©Nicole Beccai, Personal collection
Page 127: ©Collection CHRD/ Ville de Lyon. (2002, July, 29).
TICKETS de RATIONNEMENT [digital image].
Retrieved from:
http://beninois.free.fr/musee_resistance/tickets-rationnement.jpg

ISBN
978-1-3103-8994-8 (eBook)
978-1-5376-2309-2 (Paperback)
A-SIN
B0ILR80YPO (Kindle eBook)
All rights reserved

All the characters' names in this book have been changed to preserve privacy.

No part of this publication may be reproduced in any form, or by any means, electronic or mechanical, including photocopying, recording, or any information browsing, storage, or retrieval system, without permission in writing from the publisher.

Published by Claude Beccai at CreateSpace

I dedicate this work to my daughter Manuelle Frédérique who lost her war against cancer. She was a fierce and proud resister; she also knew about love. Her presence alone could inspire a room full of people.

I also want to offer it to her dear and faithful friend, Sonya Rodier, who was with her to the last moment.

Before she died in October 2015, Manuelle had read almost half of this book in progress and she approved.

Acknowledgements

I need to make a list of all the friends without which I never would have finish this work. My sister Jacqueline and her husband Willy Litzenberg who dutifully read each vignette as I was writing them, encouraging and praising, suggesting. My sister Nicole who supplied the pictures I missed, for she is the picture keeper in the family. She also read most of the vignettes by means of Google translator.

It could be that, due to the style of this manuscript, I was more in need of reassurance than with other writing experiences of mine. So, I screamed for help on Facebook. First, I begged four "Friends" (people whose posts agreed with at least some of my convictions) Betsy Busch of New York City who vouched to be honest and not meek. She was true to her words. Then, David Hunnicutt of Texas, who did a prompt review as promised and helped me by his heartfelt assessment of the work. At about the same time Dr. Lance D. Chambers from Australia, whose endorsement of my manuscript gave me more confidence, but I would be amiss not to mention the adamant supporter, I found in Marne Carmean from Los Angeles and that I promoted to Chief policewoman of the text. She even played Grand'mère when the Camille of my fancies turned mute. That is thanks to her, that I was able to write the last vignette.

Later on, I found a talented graphic artist in Jackie Chambers, she spruced up old photos of mine and made them watchable. Then, she proposed a slew of drawings, demeaning her talent to those of a seven-year-old for the purpose of enhancing the text.

Claude Beccai

I must also talk about Patricia Gall, the baroness of punctuation, with her bucket of commas, her zillions of questions, and her clear sight of where I wanted to go. All that wrapped in yards of kindness.

Now, you might think that I should have been more than satisfied, and call it quits. But no, I also formed a group of volunteers on Facebook to read a vignette at a time, under the express obligation to comment. 45 people showed up. I can't name them all, but I am deeply grateful to them all.

Contents

Acknowledgements vii
Foreword. xiii
Preface xvii
Note to the reader
   This message is only for children readers   1
   And this is for the grownup readers 2
Here I Am… 5
The consent 9
Heaven and Paradise 11
The egg 13
Body lice 15
Mustaches. 17
The wits. 19
The bunkers 21
Rutabagas 23
The Maniac 25
Collaborators and Resisters 29
A time to speak 31
The fruity man 33
Bread and the food stamps 37
Vichy 39
The rascal 41
The riding pants 43
Nightmares 45
The Swastika 47
The tantrums 49

The consultation. 51
The boobs and the painted legs 53
The rust-red dresses. 57
From under the table. 59
The laundering and losing marbles. 61
The wood stove 65
The telephone and the toilets. 67
Grand'mère disappeared. 69
Queuing for beans 71
The short wave radio 77
What happens to the dead 79
Grand'mère tells stories. 81
The shoes 85
Life is full of surprises. 87
The story. 95
Doing the N. 99
Photo Album. 101
On fire 103
My God! 107
Black the rabbit
   I will never eat a rabbit ever, ever, ever. 109
The exodus 113
Cesar my fiancè 115
How to keep warm. 121
The war at home 125
The ration tickets 127
The markets
   I know of three kinds of market. 129
The provisioning. 133
Nana, the accident 139
Winter 1942 141

The savages.......................... 145
The castle 147
Father comes back 151
Playing school...................... 153
The village is happy 157
The Germans are kaput
 but on their way 159
War is dead......................... 163
Comments........................... 167

Camille 1944

Foreword

Few things may engulf a heart with resolve nor emote concern therewithin as the frightened pleadings of a child in peril.

When, as individuals, we encounter a child in harm's way, instinctively most will act without hesitation for the safety of the child. The risk to life and limb becomes immaterial as the safety of the child becomes our sole concern; there, within but one small life, may dwell the future of all mankind.

On occasion, could it be "the rescue" comes not to the child, but from the child? An innocent smile, a kind whisper, a naive thought expressed; any and all are capable of stoking an adult's dwindling "flame within" back unto a raging fire. Acquiescence to fear amidst disaster may appear imminent and unavoidable; yet, exciting of one's will to live...the need, the instinct, the desire to assure the survival of a child ~through unknown acts or words from one incapable of defending oneself, such life forces within us may be revived and renewed.

For anyone who has experienced combative violence, as well as for all who've a desire to create, to know, to witness, to bring to being "lasting peace"; such appears as plausible and achievable when we take of our time to gaze ~but for a moment~ through the eyes of the least celebrated and most unwitting participant of any "war": a child...

...such momentary gazing is *fait accompli* through penned stories and tales expressed within *"Camille1944"*. Captivatingly articulated in the spoken ~and unspoken~ thoughts of a young French girl engulfed in the challenges of surviving a defining era of modern history; often humorous while sometimes expressively poignant, this presentation is penned in such a manner as could only a young child conceive and express. In portraying the vignettes from this seldom asserted perspective (the mind of a child in a mature world, where 'reason' by cause of war is left in absentia); the stories have been brilliantly composed by one who witnessed what may reasonably be asserted as the most significant conflict of the 20th Century ~World War II.

War takes its tolls; however, no greater toll may be paid than one levied upon a child, confused and lacking of the ability to grasp that which is occurring around them. Discovering that humanity is in fact displaying complete opposition to all she'd previously known as right or wrong...? Such experiences affecting not only the child, but the adult she will become, and all those whom her life's works will touch.

Countless crises ("wars") shall always erupt as human ideologies clash and oppose; folly unleashes wherewith the hounds of hell may ravage the innocent, absent notice of perpetration, unto the sheer and absolute epitome of crimes; the innocence of a child being stolen. As experienced recollections of war replace images of joy and happiness after such great deceptions are forced upon unsuspecting lives; the simplest words, poignantly asserted, yield profundity n'er to be surpassed in their truth: "War is a lie." (From: *"Camille 1944"*)

Paris, France: 1944, the *"city of lights"*. Long considered a stalwart of beauty, a center of creativity, a keystone of "the arts"; in opposition to the "lights", the city has seen the darkest of times as well.

Such times whereunto *"Camille"* takes our minds by sharing the stories she experienced; as if through synchronicity personified, *"Paris* and *Camille"* both 'taken' unwittingly. Compiling unbeknownst youthful coping mechanisms, *"Camille"* forms a life of happiness and sorrow entwined; tears of joy and pain appear while traversing hither and yon unto never

Camille 1944

before anticipated destinations amidst unlikely tomorrows; unforeseen confusions brought on by invaders and occupiers, a resistant strength being conceived within a child...incapable of understanding the very words but knowing of the feelings, having witnessed horrors few dare imagine. *"Camille's"* progressive trek throughout the duration gives rise to stories which captivate hearts and minds; her innocence and *joie de vivre* reviving the souls of those around her; her mind somehow finding rare beauty afloat in a sea of ugliness ~desperation overcome.

"World War Two"; a time of atrocities committed; now nearing unto becoming lost within the annals of history. The words composed and presented in *"Camille 1944"*; stories of a child's reminiscences...perhaps these words and stories may aide precluding those memories becoming forgotten. As a child may refuse to speak of what was witnessed, so too may we as a society refuse to allow repetition.

These vignettes and stories reveal a secreted portion of *"Camille's"* life. Born unto relative normalcy ~a simple life~ her life's 'interruption' is documented in a wonderfully unique form; such being, *"as from the mind of a child"*... adults seldom express with such simplistic yet shocking accuracy, the true faces of war. These words from a child, when added to the pictures they create in our minds, bring 'meaning' to life; a plethora of emotions spring forth as we are provided this rare opportunity to vicariously experience a forbidden childhood...from a perspective of innocence lost, in the confines of the reality of war.

Author Claude Beccai (born in pre WW2 Paris, France) uses words to grant us glimpses of more oft than not unspoken truths, presented through the thoughts and views of *"Camille"*. Each vignette *"Camille"* shares is profound when read by the discerning mind. Words left unspoken, scenes left descriptively not displayed; such seem to "live" between the printed lines, with such complexity physically and emotionally; survival ~essentiated by circumstance, destined unto posterity.

Claude Beccai

Having survived combative environments as an 'antagonist' (when viewed from Camille's mind, unknowing, even absent of political concern), my heart was deeply touched, my mind was inspired, my spirit began to heal as I read these truths displayed. No greater hell can exist, nor may greater beauty be conceived, than truths long ignored being brought to light as those once oppressed find liberation ~closure becoming complete through words long overdue now being told. A perspective of war as seen through eyes not allowed to remain innocent, *"Camille 1944"*; her observations, her thoughts and conclusions lent more than she could have known to the world ~a living testimony of kindness prevailing in a world wrought with disharmony and fear.

From an approach I'd not seen coming, the author (Claude Beccai: a dear friend and confidant, her wisdom and experiences abounding) imparts invaluable life lessons through *"Camille's"* words spoken, thoughts left silent, dreams revealed. Through *"Camille 1944"*, Claude touched my jaded soul; whilst sharing forbidden truths, exposing secrets long since cached, sharing parts of life few may ever truly know...and in so doing she presented *"Camille"*, who assuredly stole my heart.

An emotion shaping work of lasting importance; a journey of truths lived, and life reformed.

~

Love and kindness always,

David C C Hunnicutt

Former United States Army Captain
Former Texas Peace Officer: City of Dallas
Published Author
Currently: Seeker of truths extraordinaire ;)

Camille 1944

Preface

Claude Beccai was born in Paris, France only a few years prior to the onset of WWII. Her parents were living on the 6th floor ~formerly "maid quarters"~ of an apartment building in Paris...the city destined to soon become a pivotal location of the world wide struggle, centered in great part amidst the Western Europe theatre.

Her mother, Marcelle, was originally from the Normandy region of France. Her father, Antonio from Tuscany, had become a refugee in France after having fled the fascism devouring of Italy. These two otherwise loving people had an ongoing personal "war" regarding the virtues of butter versus olive oil; violence not being a part of their life...then came war.

Antonio was a dreamer, a reader, an idealist prone to catching colds in the malevolent Parisian weather.

Claude's mother, Marcelle, was an extremely energetic woman who had 'much better' things to do than knitting, reading or "house-wifing".

A muchly redemptive feature of life in Paris was ~pre-war~ the food. Whenever possible, which was not too often, the loving family all talked amicably over raw oysters, sea urchins, or "moules marinières"...and of course, the beauty of a plethora of wonderfully delicious French desserts.

There was joy, there was love, and there was 'bitter warring' (mainly about the above-mentioned olive oil and butter).

Claude Beccai

Later in life, Claude Beccai became married ...to an Irish crackpot / dreamer / "poet". Then, as before; there was joy, there was love, and there was 'bitter warring' (this time revolving primarily of the superior French know-how versus the Irish knack for rhymes).

Claude Beccai, having lived most of her adult life in Canada, at locations spanning shore to shore / coast to coast, now lives in Vancouver, British Columbia.

Camille 1944

Note to the reader

This message is only for children readers:

If you are a child and someone gave you this book, do not read the next two pages. They are boring. It is just a grandma who wrote them and, as you know, grandmas can be nice, but they know very little and do not know they do not know. Anyway, I did not write this book for you, because I have nothing to teach you that you do not already know. I wrote it for the grownups who have forgotten they were children and do not listen to you, because you scare them. What scares the grown-ups is the way you look at things, with wondering eyes, the way you listen and smell, the way you question everything. You see, most grownups do not want to learn anymore, they just sit on what they think they know. So, since I am a grownup, I decided to forget what I learned, magically time-travel, and for a while return to what I once was, a curious seven year old girl at a time and place I hope, you never visit. My advice, keep dreaming of pioneering on planet Mars, or hiding your pet snake under your bed, or flying with invisible wings, or making the bully that bugs you disappear.

I have a perk for you little people! You do not need to read this book page after page; you can start anywhere, skip what you do not like and finish anywhere, too. I find that fun, do not you?

Claude Beccai

And this is for the grownup readers:

For the grownups, first of all thank you for picking up this book, I hope my stories do not bore you. All I say here did truly happen to me and has shaped my way of looking at things for the better and the worse. I changed names of people for the sake of privacy, just in case they, or their descendants are still alive and are offended. Of course maniacs such as Hitler have existed. It is hard to believe that the human race can repeatedly produce, monsters of the sort, but let's not forget that these monsters are mere puppets of worse monsters who work in the shadow. They keep popping up around the world: in Brazil, in Argentina, in Saudi Arabia, in Russia and in Rumania. However I did not write this book to give a lecture in world affairs; I wrote it to give a voice to all the past, present and future war children who number in the millions, in Syria, in Africa, in Latin America, in Asia, and sadly here in North America, particularly with the Black and Aboriginal children. To do so, I returned to my three foot tall self when Europe was ablaze. I was a privileged child to be born in France, for I could have been born in Poland, or Russia or Germany where I probably would not have survived unless my parents would have been clever enough and wealthy enough to escape to more hospitable horizons.

This is not meant to be a sob story, for as a child this was my world and I just saw it as a matter of fact, nothing before and nothing after. Only the present counts for a child. When sad, the child is sad forever, even if in grownup time it only lasts ten minutes. There is no chronology in this work, because a child does not have a sense of time, or rather the child has a different sense of time. The child follows the feelings rather than the timing, and it is out of his or her need to sort out the events occurring around him/her that the child constructs reality. We need to return to this perspective. The weight of our long grownup experience tends to cloud our judgment.

Camille 1944

    I hope I succeeded in giving a voice to the child I once was, that some will listen and befriend her, I also hope this will encourage them to reconnect with their own childhood as there is much to gain in doing so.

Camille 1944

Here I Am...

It is 1944 in occupied France. I am seven and a half but I will be eight pretty soon, grownups call me "a proper brat", which is not nice. But it does not matter because I think all adults are retarded apart from my grandmother and sometimes my mother. The Germans ¬you can also say the Krauts, the Boches, the Fritzes, but be careful not aloud¬ are mean people that you must stay away from, otherwise they put you in ugly trains for cows and send you directly to concentrated camp where they fry you and eat you for breakfast. (Grand'mère told me so). Concentrated is not a new word for me, I already know about concentrated milk, so instead it is concentrated camps. These ones are also called Dachau. Concentrated milk is milk that you can make smaller by pushing on it, so concentrated camps are where you make people smaller. Grand'mère says that the Germans are good at doing things like that. They also invented concentrated carrots that we call dehydrated carrots. Those are only good to make a soup that does not taste as good as the Before-The-War soups. That is what Grand'mère says and I believe her. She is right most of the time. I guess when the people come back from concentrated camps we will have to let them soak a long time in warm water so that they will look more like big people again.

We have gone from Paris, where there is not much food, to a village in the center of France, where there is lots of food. The villagers say they are happy to see us and most of them are nice, but not the red hair girl because she made a face at me. I have to remember to pinch her hard the first chance I get.

5

Claude Beccai

I am the oldest of three. I have two sisters, the first one is five, her name is Justine, she calls herself Just-Justine and we do too, I like her but she does not say a lot because she stutters and she prefers to listen to music, the younger one is four that one is Nadine but we call her Nana. Nana is always laughing but she does not know much. Both are kind of slow if you want my opinion but I am supposed to protect them since I am so much older, a difficult job especially with the four year old; she believes just about anything, does not know about the Fritzes or the concentrated camps, or even about thistles that make bumps on your fingers and itch for a long time after. It is normal since she is so young. Grand'mère says they will be okay later on and only laughs when I complain. I am getting old, I am seven already, and like Grand'mère says, "I feel the years upon my shoulders." I must be responsible because I have reached the Age of Reason. Grand'mère has reached the Age of Wisdom. The Age of Reason is when you can think things for yourself. It is true that I can do that. I asked Mother in what age she was; she said she was at the Age of Slaving. I do not know what she means, but Grand'mère laughed, so it must be a grownup joke that I cannot understand. Grand'mère says that I am a tireless reasoning machine. I am not sure what she means. Even if I have not gone to school yet because the doctor said it would be better if I do not, I can read, write and count up to a thousand and one. I could count more if I tried harder but it gets very boring after a while. Mother keeps all the wooden matches she is using so I learned to count, add and subtract with those used up matches. I like doing that. Just-Justine can count up to twenty but sometimes she forgets some numbers. Nana can only count up to ten, that's all but she does not mind. I mind, I want to know it all. I want to reach the Age of Wisdom fast. Wisdom means you know it all like Grand'mère. The other day a man, a friend of Mother said to me, "You're quite a little know-it-all, aren't you!" The way he said it, I could see that he did not think that is was a good thing. I do not care because I did not like him either; he has not reached the age of reason even if he is much, much older than I am.

Almost all the grownups who see me tell my parents that I should be tamed. Taming is what you do to a lion, when you want the lion to jump through hoops in a circus. Normally lions do not like jumping through hoops. They must be whipped into it; I saw one in a circus once with Grand'mère.

The way the grownups look when they say I should be tamed I can see they wish to whip me themselves. I am lucky that Mother and Father do not believe in taming small people like me.

Camille 1944

The consent

Nana broke my doll the other day. She had already broken hers and my mother let her have mine since I do not play with it. All the same this is not a good reason because I did not consent. Consent is a word I like. It means that nobody can do anything to you if you do not say yes first. I think the German soldiers do not know this word. It makes a lot of sense since it is a French word and they do not speak like we do. So they know nothing about consent. That is why they put people they do not know in cattle trains without their consent.

We travelled in cattle trains from Paris. Sometimes we had to change the train in the middle of the night until we arrived at this village where we are now, but it was with our French consent. It took four days because the train stopped a lot, and some people brought us food and some milk. When the train stopped, we were not supposed to make any noise and only talked in each other's ear. When the train was running we could shout and laugh. We slept on bales of hay. It tickled a lot and made you scratch all over.

When the train slowed down, it made a hissing sound that hurts your ears. There were also big clanking noises when the train would start up again. Trains also make a lot of smoke and smell but we could not see too much since there were only little slits between planks and no windows. I love trains. When another train would pass in the other direction, we could not see who was in it. Besides, we were not allowed to look. All the same, this was fun, except my mother was always crying and very sad. She only smiled a little when we made funny faces to wipe the sadness off her face.

Heaven and Paradise

My mother now says we are in Heaven. I think she hasn't got it right, for there are peaches and cherries but no apples. And my grandmother said there is an apple tree in Heaven. There are also only two naked people in Heaven, a man and a woman (that part is funny because it is not proper to show your bum). The lady's name is Eve and her brother is called Adam. Eve is the one who talks to snakes. This did not make God happy, so he sent both of them downstairs and ordered them to dress up because it was cold. I do not understand why God does not like the snake. Since he made everything, that means he also made the talking snake.

Talking snakes, my foot! I do not believe a word of that, of course. I am too old for that kind of fairy tale. I saw a snake once and it could not talk at all. It only could bite if you let it.

I will not tell Grand'mère though because I think she just wants to see if I believe in talking snakes but I will tell the story to Nana, my younger sister. She believes anything.

Grownups can never get their stories straight.

Grand'mères are not grownups. They have large bosoms and even bigger behinds, they dress in black, wear glasses, sit around and tell very interesting stories even when they are not true and I love mine all the way to the sky. Grand'mère does not think I am a brat but a clever funny girl. I believe she is the only one who got it right.

Camille 1944

The egg

The other day, a farmer's daughter brought us twenty four eggs; twenty four is the same as two dozen. That was so very nice. We each ate a whole egg. This is not like in Paris. I remember my mother had been so excited she had been given one egg and while she cooked it, we climbed up on a chair and watched it boil four minutes. And then we had to sit very quietly while my mother gave the three of us each a spoonful of the delicious egg.

When I am a grownup, I will only eat eggs, cherries and peaches. These are the best! Of course, this is only if we can lick the Germans and the fascists. In Paris they are the ones eating all the eggs and the cherries.

Camille 1944

Body lice

My father is hiding somewhere fighting the fascists, but I cannot tell anyone about that. One night, when we were still in Paris, he came home in the middle of the night. He was full of body lice because he had been hiding in dirty places. So my mother did not want him to come in the house until he took a bath. She filled a big bucket with warm water and he had to wash and scrub his body with a big brush and a smelly soap. Then he had to shave his hair and his beard before we could kiss him, that made us giggle because he looked so funny. I do not have hair growing on my face, only on top of my head like my mother and Grand'mère, but I know a woman who has hair on her face and I am sure she shaves like my father because I can see tiny black dots all over her cheeks just like on my father's cheeks. I know she is a woman because she wears a skirt and her name is Madame Violette. Violette is a girl's name and we have to call her Madame. Only girls and women are named after flowers, I do not know why.

Grand'mère says it is because girls are pretty like flowers, I do not think so, Madame Violette is not pretty and she does not smell good at all. I do not know many boys because I only have sisters and when a sister is a boy then she is not your sister anymore she is your brother.

Camille 1944

Mustaches

You cannot say that a boy is pretty. You can only say that he is handsome, I do not know why, I think Father is a lot prettier with hair on top of his head and I like so much his mustache, because it moves when he talks and when he smiles. Men do not cry but once I saw my father cry, it made me sad all the way down to my toes even so I did not know why he was crying. I would like to have a mustache too. Sometimes I use a pen to draw one under my nose and watch it move as I make faces in front of the mirror, Nana and Just-Justine like it too, and laugh a lot when I do it. Mother gets upset and sends me to scrub it off. She just does not like mustaches; maybe that's why she asked Father to shave. I took Father's razor and shaved the cat's whiskers to make my mother happy. It was very difficult to do but all it did was make Mother mad at me. She screamed at Grand'mère saying that she

did not know what to do with me. I was scared she would send me to concentrated camp to be cooked in the big German oven,

Claude Beccai

like in the story of the witch with Hansel and Gretel. Grand'mère made me read it. You should read it, too. I like Gretel, because she is the one who was clever and kicked the bad witch into the oven. Hansel is like Nana, he is a lamb and that is no good when you meet bad wolves or mean witches. Maybe the Nazis are the children of the witch, they did not learn how to laugh and play hopscotch. They only learned how to eat people.

I went to hide under the bed until she forgot about it.

Camille 1944

The wits

Mother forgets about things, she says she is losing her wits. I do not know what wits are, but they are very important to her. I would like to know where to find them for her, except I do not know where to look, even though I know every corner of this tiny house. The Paris house was much bigger, but she did not lose her wits so much there. I will have to ask Grand'mère what wits look like and ask if she has some. If she has, then maybe she could lend some to Mother. If I had wits I would give them all to her because I would not know what to do with them anyway. I think Mother is scared, I know about scare because I am scared a lot. I am scared that Mother will not love me anymore; I am scared that Father will not come back ever; I am scared the bombs will fall on our house by mistake and break Nana into lots of pieces; I am scared that the German soldiers will put me in the bad train alone without Mother and Nana and Just-Justine.

Grand'mère says that it is normal to be scared, but what is really important is to know that you are scared. I know I am scared because this is when I feel stiff all over my body. It starts with my back, then goes down to my legs until I cannot move anymore.

Camille 1944

The bunkers

Scared when planes full of bombs would fly over in Paris, and we had to run to hide in the basements. Mother would carry Nana, Just-Justine was supposed to hold on Mother's skirt to the left while I held on the right. The basement of our building was not safe, so we had to run all the way up the street to another building. The siren was blaring, and the noise of the planes was so loud I could not hear Nana crying, and she is a loud crier. There were men with a special hat and a lantern; they were called the Passive Defense men. These alerts were always happening at night. Once I was so scared I could not move anymore and one of these men carried me. He smelled of tobacco that was good because it reminded me of Father, so I was not scared anymore, I became all soft again.

In the basement there were lots of people I did not know. Some were crying, some others were talking and making jokes, I know they were jokes because other people were laughing, but I did not understand what they were talking about.

There were also other children. We were asked to be quiet, so we only looked and listened. Mother was holding us very tight and I could feel she was shaking, that is strange because it was not cold in there.

One boy sitting across from me had his legs quite apart, and I could see through the legs in his pants that his in- between-legs was not like mine. Until now, I only recognized boys because they have short hair and wear short pants, I wished it was not so dark in the basement and I could see better. So I smiled at him and he let me play with his marbles. His name is Gerard. I kissed him. He looked kind of scared even though I smiled. Nana came over and kissed him too. She always does what I do, and that is very annoying. Just-Justine never talks. She lets me do the talking, maybe because she stutters and it takes her a long time to say something. I really like Just-Justine, she always listens when I talk, just like Grand'mère and does not think I am a brat. Maybe she will not become a grownup; she will become a Grandma right away.

Camille 1944

Rutabagas

French grownups hate rutabagas, Mother and Grand'mère hate them, too. They say it is food for pigs. They talk about potatoes that the Germans steal from us to leave us only turnips and rutabagas. I like turnips and rutabagas, but I do not say it to anybody except to Just-Justine, because grownups would think I am not really French. If you are French, you must hate turnips. I do not care because I will never be a French grownup. And I will not be a German grownup either.

Camille 1944

The Maniac

The Germans have a big chief, who is German too. His name is Hitler. I saw a picture of him, he wears a mustache like Father. But Father says he is a maniac. I do not know what a maniac is, so one day to show people how bright I am, I say Hitler is a maniac. Mother came over, took me under her arms and locked me in the bedroom. I threw a tantrum, because it was unfair. She never did that when Father said it. I kicked the door as hard as I could until Grand'mère came to see me. She explained that there are things that cannot be said in front of everyone. Then a man, who said he was a friend of Father, knocked at the door of the bedroom, sat on the bed and told me that one can do a lot of damage by talking too much in front of people one did not know very well. These days, he said, even children had to grow up fast.

The problem is that I do not want to grow up. I can deal with being a brat, even a little pest, an impertinent know-it-all, but I do not want to be a grownup, or getting to be one. This man smiled at me and asked if Father really said that Hitler was a maniac. I did not like looking at his eyes as he was asking, so while Grand'mère was holding my hand hard, I told him I made it up because I only wanted to know what a maniac is. Grand'mère stopped squishing my hand, that's how I knew that I had answered correctly. The man asked who used the word maniac and for whom. I said Father said Madame Granet is a maniac because she never stops talking, and I am a maniac too, and maybe Hitler is, because he talks a lot on the radio.

Claude Beccai

A maniac is a collaborator and a collaborator is worse than a German, Father said that and that is the only thing Father and Grand'mère agree on.

Collaborators and Resisters

The collaborators are the ones who can eat potatoes and legs of lamb. I do not know what a leg of lamb is, but I know it is something that you eat that is very good. I have two legs but I am not a lamb. I have girl's legs. The resisters are the ones we should like because they are Father's friends. Resisters cannot find tobacco and have to hide all the time. It was not like this Before-The-War. Before-The-War everybody could eat potatoes and legs of lamb. They could also smoke as many cigarettes as they wanted. I do not remember Before-The-War. I think I was three then, Just-Justine was one, and Nana was just born,. I was so much older than they were, I could speak and run; I had to teach them.

Father one day came home very happy; he had tobacco seeds in his pocket. He planted the seeds in a little pot and told Mother not to forget to water the seeds. It is fun to watch them grow, but it is very slow. When people we do not know well come for a visit, we must hide the pot under the kitchen sink until they are gone. The pot is a secret. I like secrets. When the plant is big and gets large leaves, then Father will smoke them. I do not know why but I like the smell of tobacco, because it smells like Father and his friends. Apart from Mother, Father only has men friends. Grand'mère is not his friend.

Camille 1944

A time to speak

I wish I could be like Nana because everybody says she is cute. I would love to be cute so people would like me, and Mother would not roll her eyes all the time when she looks at me and say, "Camille why do not you shut up for a bit!" Grand'mère says I should turn my tongue one hundred times before I speak. I tried that, but I cannot get to more than 67. Sixty-seven is the longest I can wait to speak. Even so, I can count all the way to a thousand and one. Words come jumping out of my mouth on their own.

1, 2, 3, 4, ... 45, 46,....66 Doing what Grand'mère told me to do but it takes too long...

Grand'mère says there is a time to speak your mind, but now is not the time. "When is the time?" I asked. She says, "Before-The-War was the time." And she sighs. When she sighs her bosom goes up and then down. It would be fun to have a big bosom that goes up and down. Grand'mère says, "Plenty of time, do not rush into it. Bosom can be bothersome." Still, when rope jumping, it would be super fun; Grand'mère does not do rope jumping because of her bunion. Maybe I could put peaches inside my dress; I will try that when Mother is not watching because she never likes my ideas.

29

Camille 1944

The fruity man

I do not only talk, I listen a lot, too. I want to learn everything there is to learn and this is not easy, because when I ask questions either people laugh at me, or get mad, and even tell me that I am vicious. Like the other day, a woman who knows my mother, she works at the bakery, she sells bread and flans; Mother calls her the baker's wife. She said that she thinks the priest is fruity. The priest is the man who wears a long black dress with buttons all the way down and a strange black hat with four wings on top. He walks while reading a book, but wears a white lacy long shirt when he says the mass, (I know because I am the only one of the family who is supposed to go to church on Sundays. Grand'mère says it is because we must show that we are of good faith, and my sisters are too young, my mother too busy, and Grand'mère has a bunion that hurts when she walks.)

    1, 2, 3, 4, ... 45, 46,....61 I try...

    I have to go to church on Sundays but I do not mind; actually, it is interesting. The church is beautiful – it is big and you can only speak in a low voice, except when you sing. Then everyone's voices go up to the ceiling and come back to you like another voice that fills your ears. There are bells on top of the church. The bells can ring with different sounds depending on why they ring. There is a man who is the bell ringer. He is the only one who knows which rope to pull and which song he wants the bells to sing. On Sundays it is a happy song, but when someone dies it is a sad slow song. Also, the bells tell you what time it is, for example, if it is three a clock, the bells ring only three times politely.

In the church there is a fountain just as you come in through the big door. This is where you can wash the one finger of your right hand, because God does not have enough water to wash all your hand. It is the priest who fills the fountain and he does not just have that to do. If you dipped your whole hand, it would mean that you are not appreciative of the priest's effort to clean you. Appreciative means that you know what is good for you.

After you pass the fountain there are lots of chairs, but you cannot move the chairs because they are stuck to the floor. Then you walk quietly and sit where there is enough room for your bum. Most of the time, the person who will be beside you smiles quietly at you, and you are supposed to smile back but not talk. That is to show that you are civilized. That means you have manners. I forgot to tell you that if you are a lady or a girl you must wear a hat when you are in a church, Boys and men must not wear a hat. I do not know why. The god in that church only likes men's hair.

If you do not know what is happening, it does not matter because you can always look at the windows. Instead of curtains, they have beautiful pictures painted on them, where all the men wear long dresses. There are pictures of Jesus with long dresses and long hair. Maybe he does not like to wear dresses because he never laughs or smiles.

You do not just stand. Sometimes you have to kneel, sometimes you sit, and other time you say things, as if you are answering the priest. Also, all of a sudden people start lining up all the way to the little gate. Then they kneel down, open their mouth and get a flat round thing in it that is called a wafer. Then you make a cross with your fingers and you are supposed to say: "In the name of the father, the son and the holy spirit, So be it". (I do not know why but I am not allowed to get a wafer. I wish I could.)

1, 2, 3, 4, ... 45, 46,....69 WOW! I made it to 69 I'm getting better...

Camille 1944

"Fruity" is a new word for me. I wonder if it is because he smells of apple sauce, or because he wears a long dress even if he has the voice of a man. Or it can be because he wears that ugly hat that no other man wears. I will try to talk to the baker's wife, but I must be careful with my questions. She says she knows a lot because it is her husband who makes the wafers since the war started.

Camille 1944

Bread and the food stamps

The baker's wife is nice with me, because The Village adopted us, and when I go to buy bread with my money and the tickets, she only takes the money but not the tickets. Also the bread is white in The Village; in Paris you could only get black bread even with tickets. The Germans made us have tickets, so many per person; if you do not have tickets plus the money, you cannot get bread I think that is because they do not want us to get fat. When you are fat, you take more space and leave the Germans with less space. I wonder if the Germans are going to see that Grand'mère has a big bum and stop giving her bread tickets. I know a fat girl in The Village, she is ten years old and she always pushes me, so I pull my tongue at her and make ugly faces. As soon as I feel stronger I will kick her bum.

Vichy

Grand'mère says that it is all because of the rascals in Vichy. They are a bunch of collaborators, sold out to the Boches. I do not know what that means! I do not want to grow up but I want people to think that I know what I am talking about. This is not because I am not big, that I am an idiot. You can only say Boches when no one is listening, and I do not count. You are not supposed to say the word "Boche" the same way you say German. When you say "Boche" it must sound as if you are spitting, and right away people know that you do not like Germans. If you want to have legs of lamb and silk stockings, you must show that you like the Germans.

Vichy, Grand'mère says, used to be a pretty city where she went to take baths, drink bubbly water and listen to pretty ladies sing fun songs like "Le Temps des Cerises". Grand'mère knows that song by heart. And so do I because she taught me.

Camille 1944

The rascal

In Paris there was another rascal, Monsieur Henri. He was the one who knew about The Village and about the train we took. Grand'mère gave him some of her bracelets and necklaces and he accompanied us to the train. We carried lots of heavy stuff, not Nana but even Just-Justine carried stuff. We each had a bag on our back with important things, like our doll, two books and the used matches for counting.

I was allowed to take my knuckle-bones, I am getting good at it. It is a game for both boys and girls. Marbles are mostly for boys but I like that, too. Mother does not want me to have marbles because she says I keep forgetting them at the wrong place and they make Grand'mère trip. This is not nice because she has a big bunion on one foot that makes her walk funny. One foot is okay but she is kind of slow to put the sick one down. She says it is because she ate too many rutabagas for her own good.

I did not know rutabagas could do that. I will have to be more careful. I do not want to have a bunion like hers.

Mother lost two teeth; she says it is because she carried too many children too fast. I have also lost my two front teeth, (Mother's lost teeth were in the back of her mouth). I only carry Nana sometimes, she is very heavy but I do not carry her fast. I should have grown other big teeth but I have not yet. Grand'mère says it is because we do not eat properly and I look too pale. So now we are in The Village, Mother and I will grow our teeth back.

1, 2, 3, 4, ... 45, 46,....72 I'm proud of myself...

Claude Beccai

Grand'mère says that sometimes rascals can be useful, but the ones in Vichy are not useful. There is a big cheese now in Vichy and it is called Maréchal Pétain. I have eaten camembert once but never Maréchal Pétain even once. I know many words that mean German: boches, fritzes, krauts, green mice (green mice is only for the women dressed in green, that are meaner than mean, everybody says so), We also call them "Curlies" that is to make fun of them since they do not have curly hair, just blond with straight very short hair. The worst of all are the Gets-Tapo. Tapo must be one of the poor miscreants Grand'mère is always talking about. All these words, you should not say them aloud even in front of someone you know except Grand'mère or Father. Mother makes mean eyes when you say them, I know because I tried it. I have black curly hair so I am not a boche. "Boche" is a dirty word like bum and fuck- you. The Gets-Tapo soldiers are all in black like the priest in The Village, but they wear pants not dresses and they do not have the same funny hat either.

Camille 1944

The riding pants

When you are in the metro in Paris, you see a lot of Boches. They have big brown shiny boots all the way up to under their knees and higher they have trousers that are much larger at their thighs; this is so that they can grow fat on French food. When I explained that to Grand'mère, she laughed so hard that she even cried. She said, "if the Boches do not kill me you will, little one". I do not want to kill Grand'mère, I like her too much. And I do not want her to go to paradise, because she cannot eat apples anyway since she has a toothache. Peaches are okay, not the pits, of course. All the same, I do not know if she is making a joke. I do not understand many jokes except the one about knock, knock, who is there? Grand'mère says that it does not matter, because I am a twenty four hour joke every day, even when I sleep, because I also talk when I sleep.

Camille 1944

Nightmares

I have big scary nightmares.

One I remember, because I dreamed it many times. There is a big elephant, with two long mean teeth, that is crushing everything he is walking on. With its big teeth he is eating all the potatoes and legs of lamb. He also stepped on Mother and Father with his big paws.

I am hiding behind the armchair with Just-Justine and Nana and I have to tell them, even though I do not want to, that now I am their mother but they do not like that.

The elephant looks like the one in my book of animals, his name is Fridolin. Funny because this is what Monsieur Henri calls the Germans. (Monsieur Henri is a real Parisian and he speaks Parisian French with lots of funny words that Mother does not want me to use, but it makes Grand'mère laugh.)

Claude Beccai

We were very afraid; I still am when I wake up. I cry until morning, Mother holding me tight on her lap crying with me. Since we arrived in The Village I do not dream as much.

Camille 1944

The Swastika

When you are in the Metro you must not look at German soldiers' eyes. This is not too difficult because they are so much bigger than me. When I look straight I see up to their belt. But even though, Grand'mère told me not to, sometimes I make as if I am not looking but I look. They have strange decorations on their sleeves and on their jacket collars they wear a sign – Grand'mère calls it an insignia. It looks like a plus sign with minus signs on each end of the plus sign. Maybe it is because they are fruity like The Village priest. But it would be a different kind of fruits. The Nazis' kind. You are not supposed to talk to Nazis ever. They are the mean kind. They eat people with black curly hair.

1, 2, 3, 4, ... 45, 46,....60 only to sixty because I have to say what I want to say before somebody shuts me up

Once I looked at the insignia, because I wanted to draw some in my book. The soldier looked at me directly, so I could see he had seen that I too, was looking at him, and he winked and smiled. I hid my face in Mother's lap. Maybe he was doing what the farmers do when they want to kill and eat a chicken. They use a funny soft voice and say: "Here, chicken, chicken, come to me, you beauty." I do not know how it would feel to be in a German belly. Maybe he would get a belly ache, like what I get when I eat too fast.

Claude Beccai

On a sheet of newspaper, I drew a whole bunch of the Nazi's insignia, to make sure I could do it. It was not too difficult but I wanted to have it exactly right. When Mother saw it she got very upset, tore the paper to pieces, and threw all the little pieces in the fireplace. I was so surprised that I forgot to have a tantrum.

The tantrums

I have lots of tantrums; They always start when I cannot get what I want when what I want is reasonable. Like the day I wanted to climb all the way up the Eiffel Tower. It is only stairs, I can do it with my two good legs and Grand'mère with her bunion was not with us.

With a tantrum, I always start screaming to the top of my voice, and I do not care who looks at me. Really I want everyone to know that I am upset. Then I stamp my feet real, real hard still screaming. Then Mother says, "Not again, stop that immediately, little brat!" This is when I fall down on the ground and start rolling. It hurts but I do not care, then I do not remember anymore why I am screaming but it feels good, so I keep doing it until I get really sick. I spit and vomit.

I want everyone to know that I am enraged. The more people around, the louder I am because it makes Mother ashamed to have a daughter like me. I want her to feel as badly as I feel.

Camille 1944

The consultation

One day, Mother asked the doctor for a consultation. A consultation is when a doctor comes to your house, listens to your chest, and puts a stick in your mouth while you say, "Haaaaaaa". The doctor is Doctor Morel. He is a big man, bigger than Father, he smells of talc.

Mother tells him that she is not sure anymore if she can handle me. And then she talks of my tantrums.

The doctor listens real hard then he asks me if I have a pain somewhere.

I do not.

He asks me then if there is something I want.

I start to cry because the doctor reminds me of Father, even though he does not look like him.

The doctor says, "It is alright, you can tell me in my ear".

I like secrets, I hide my mouth with my hand and in a very low voice so Mother cannot hear I say: "I want Father to be home, I want to say Boche, Nazi, maniac and fuck you aloud. I want people to hear me."

Then the doctor smiles and said you can say it to me, how about you shout it right now.

So I try. First, not too loud while I look at Mother.

She says, "No, Doctor!" and puts her hand over her mouth.

The doctor says, "Louder!"

And I do it louder and louder till I scream. It feels so good, it makes me giggle. This is a good game. I am the only one to laugh.

But the Doctor smiles at me and says, "Now whenever you feel like doing it again, just shout and I will come see you"

He leaves and does not want Mother to pay for the consultation because he had such a good time with me.

I think I am in love with the doctor; I will marry him because he is not like a lot of grownups who tell Mother I should be tamed. All the same, that is the last time I saw him.

Grand'mère said they caught him. He is a goner. There are lots of goners. One day, you see them and have a chat with them, next day they are gone. Goners...

Camille 1944

The boobs and the painted legs

The farmer's daughter came back the other day. She brought us more peaches and apricots. Mother says she is a nice girl, but I do not think so because she has a larger bosom than Mother, but it is not as big as Grand'mère's. So she is a grownup like Mother. While Mother was not listening, she was putting the fruits in a bin we have, to keep food, because of the rats. Rats are like the Germans if you let them, they eat all your food. But it is easier with rats because you are allowed to kill them.

I asked the girl-woman if she liked her bosom. She looked at me; I guessed she did not understand the word, "bosom". So without touching, I showed her what I meant.

"Oh" she said, "You mean my boobs", and she put her fingers to her mouth.

That means that this is another word that one cannot say aloud but I like it. Then the girl-woman asks me to tell her things about Paris. I have to be careful what I say – I remember Grand'mère's warnings – but I am very pleased that she thinks I am worth asking. I first ask how old she is, and she says she is almost sixteen. So I tell her that I am almost twelve.

"What do you want to know?" I ask like Mother would do.

She says: "Everything, tell me about the Metro."

So I sit on the highest chair we have, I cross my legs and put my hands flat on my thighs like Mother because it looks more grownup.

Nana and Just-Justine are playing under the table.

Claude Beccai

1, 2, 3, 4,.... 45, 46 ...68 I counted longer this time because I wanted to have a glass of water and there will be a lot to say...

I start explaining that to get in the Metro you must go down a lot of stairs and you must have a ticket. When you get to where the trains stop that looks like a long long tunnel, you give your ticket to a sitting man with a special cap on his head with RTP written on it. He has a neat hole punching tool in his hand. He gives the ticket back to you with a hole in it; that means you become a true metro traveler. You must not lose that ticket until you are out of the Metro. Sometimes a man comes in the Metro and you have to show the ticket. If you lost it, then they put your mother in jail and make her pay lots of money. I do not want Mother to go to jail, so I hang tight to my ticket. Nana and Just-Justine do not need to have a ticket because they are too young. You only pay if you are six and well behaved. Well behaved is when you never say what you think. Sometimes I can do t, sometimes I cannot.

It stinks down there, but you must make as if you do not smell the smell. Mother says it is the worst place to catch lice. So you must make very tight braids with your hair. Lice do not care for braids. Soap is difficult to find, The Germans take it, too, and that is why a lot of French people stink and are not very clean. If lice catch you, your mother must wash your hair with a terrible liquid that comes in a bottle. It stings even though it has a nice name. It is called Marie Rose.

Now I am going to tell you about the painted legs...

Mother comes back with five apricots in her hands and gives me one, and one to each of my sisters, and then she puts the other two on the table. I like apricots, I like the name, too. I will call my broken doll Apricot even if it is the name of a fruit and not of a flower. I do not think the priest should have the name of a fruit even if he is fruity, because he looks more like an eggplant.

Camille 1944

Eggplants are not fruits. They are village vegetables. Mother sits nicely and smiles at the girl-woman that she calls Marguerite. That's another flower name.

Once I asked Grand'mère why I did not get a flower name. She said that's because they would have had to call me Thistle and they wanted to give me a second chance.

Then she laughed. It must be a joke. Grand'mère always laughs at her own jokes. That's how I know it is a joke.

Marguerite tells Mother that she has pretty legs. I do not think that is a good way to start talking to my mother, but Mother smiles and looks at her legs. I look too, but nothing has changed. She has done this morning what she does almost every morning. She paints her legs with a brown liquid that make her legs browner, then very, very carefully she paints a line in the back all the way from her ankles to her thighs. That's what all the women do in Paris to make believe they wear silk stockings. Silk stockings are only for collaborators.

One day Monsieur Henri brought a pair to my mother, but Grand'mère said she should not accept them because they were suspicious. Until now, I did not know about suspicious stockings, so I looked at them really hard. But since I do not know what suspicious is, I could not find anything that could explain suspicious. Only that suspicious is a word that you can say aloud. It is not an angry word. If you paint your legs like this, people can see you are a real lady like Mother. The line at the back means it is the seam of the stocking. It looks more like the true thing and you are a truer Parisian lady. So men can look at you and wink. Even Father thinks it is pretty.

So Mother asked Marguerite if she ever painted her legs, like so. Marguerite giggles and says no with her head.

Mother asks me to go get the paint and the little stick for the seam. The seam is painted with a darker brown. Mother tells Marguerite to bare her legs. She will show her how. Marguerite's

53

under feet are really dirty and her toe nails are black. Yet Mother makes as if it is not so. If it was me, she would send me to scrub immediately.

Since that time many girl-women come to see mother with eggs, vegetables and fruits and talk a long time with mother while we play under the table. Grand'mère made more paint with the skin of walnuts for the girls 'legs. Grand'mère said one should not underestimate the effort it took her since it is bringing us more fruits and eggs. Did you know that if you wrap eggs in paper they will keep much longer? So if the farm girls get tired of painting their legs, we will still have eggs for a long time. Mother used the pages of Nana's only book to wrap the eggs and Nana cried a long time. I was sad for her, too, because Nana does not have many things and what she gets is always used up. Since she is the youngest and the smallest when she gets something, it is because I and later Just-Justine grew out of it. Except for the red dresses, but that was a long time ago.

Camille 1944

The rust-red dresses

When Father decided to leave us to fight the Nazis, he wanted to bring with him a photo of Mother and the three of us together, so that he would always remember why he was fighting.

Mother said that she would not have a family portrait without her and us wearing something chic. It is Grand'mère who found the material. Even though she thought Father was a Triple-Fool, she said she believed in happiness. So she brought this rust-red material and the name of a seamstress who could do wonders with it. That is how the three of us got a new dress at the same time. Mother did too, but she never got to wear it. It was a beautiful dress with large flowers, but I was so impressed with it I decided to cut some of the flowers to offer them to Mother. I did it so she would be happy, but she cried a long time. I was four then and did not know better.

Camille 1944

From under the table

1, 2, 3, 4, …. 45, 46,…..60 It is time to talk about something else that's interesting…

If we promise to be very quiet and do not make a fuss, when visitors come we can play under the table. The house we live in is not very big. It has only two rooms. The one very dark without a window is where we all sleep, and the front one is where we eat – it has a window where you can see out on the street. It used to be the house of a man who looked after horses before he died. Nana and Just-Justine sleep on a straw mattress on the floor, I sleep on a cushion someone gave us, and Grand'mère and Mother sleep in a bed together.

There is no electricity and no water in our house. Someone gave us a carbide lamp to see at night. A carbide lamp gives us a lot of light but it is noisy. First you have to put some little white pellets on the bottom, and then you put water in the compartment on top. The water falls in drops on the pellets; then, you must turn a little wheel outside and strike a match. It does not smell very good. Nana, Just-Justine and even I are not allowed to touch it, only Mother and Grand'mère can touch it. Sometimes it explodes and we have to throw the lamp in the middle of the street. It is super scary but fun too, in a way. Do not tell Mother.

For water we have a big pail that we are allowed to fill from the well outside the house across the street. First you hook the pail handle to a long rope then you throw the pail down the well. It is deep, deep, deep. The pail fills very fast and you pull up on the rope that is rolling on a wheel. When the pail is out of the well, you bend and catch it carefully so you do not spill the water. I cannot do that, it is too heavy. I tried it once but I got all wet from the water I spilled not on purpose. We have to be extra careful not to dirty our clothes because it is hard for Mother to wash clothes.

Carbide Lamp ©Klaus D. Peter (modified)

Camille 1944

The laundering and losing marbles

When Mother and Grand'mère wash clothes, it is fun to watch, but they do not like us to laugh. First you get two, three or four buckets of water, and then you make sure that a good healthy fire burns in the stove, because you need warm water. You soak the clothes and you must beat them hard so the dirt is scared and goes away. After that you can rinse in cold water. You wring them one by one and hang them to dry on cords that are stretched across the eating room, because in this village house we do not have an outside. It drips all over the table and the floor and Mother must bend down to go under it. Sometimes Mother cries when the washing is going on, so we hug her and tell her we love her. She pats our heads and keeps on crying.

She says: "Little ones, do not worry, it is not your fault."

If it is not our fault then it is the war's fault. It is because of the Germans, I get really mad, and I do not want anyone to hurt Mother. When I grow up I will kill them all like we do with

the rats. From now on, I will eat all the turnips on my plate even if I am not hungry anymore. I will grow so tall that I will be able to kick all the meanies right in the butt and they won't be able to kick me back. I want it to be Before-The-War and I will buy Mother all the legs of lamb and silk stockings she likes.

Grand'mère told Mother that it is extremely important that she does not lose her marbles. The way she said it I knew she was not joking, but I did not know Mother had marbles. They must be well hidden because I never saw them. I wonder if they are in the little bag she always keeps in her purse.

Grand'mère said: "You have three beautiful angels. Now we can eat and have a roof over our heads. Let's rejoice at our good fortune!"

That makes Mother cry even more. Nana and Just-Justine are crying too. I cannot cry, and I feel as stiff as if I am made out of wood. When Mother cries, I get so scared that she will leave us because she is fed up with us. Grand'mère sends us outside to get some wood for the fire, so I cannot hear what more she said. But when we come back with the wood – I carry three pieces, Just-Justine carries two and Nana carries only one – Mother is smiling again. Grand'mère says she has more than one trick in her bag, and it is true she is like the magician we saw once in the Bois de Boulogne. He turned one piece of burning paper into a handkerchief. I really love Grand'mère and we three run to kiss Mother.

I forgot what I was saying. Grand'mère says it is very important to remember, so that people will know and do not do the same mistakes again. Importance is a word I am not sure about. Sometimes I think one story is important and Grand'mère says it is not. Mother does not think, because she is too busy with other things, and Grand'mère says I am the one who must remember because she won't last long so I must be her memory. When I tell her that I will always remember the red hair girl who directly stuck her tongue at me, she says it is trivial – that means not important – but the rutabagas are important! Go figure...I do not always understand Grand'mère. Then Grand'mère did a strange thing. She hugged me very tight and said in my ears: "Thank you, for keeping me almost sane, little one."

I do not know what it means but I am sure it is a compliment and a secret just by the way she said it.

Camille 1944

The wood stove

1, 2, 3, 4, ... 45, 46,....69... Counted real fast this time...

Under the table, Nana sings a song to MY doll and usually she falls asleep before the doll does, Just-Justine plays with her toes and sings songs she heard on the radio. She does not stutter when she sings. I look and listen. When you look, you see. You see feet and knees mostly, sometimes hands, too. The people around the table are important people from The Village. They said they came to ask Mother and Grand'mère what is it they need. The Village wants to help. Mother made me promise that I would not talk. She said if I did, she would abandon me or throw me to the rats. It is too bad because I would have said that we needed a pair of silk stockings and ten legs of lamb from Before-The-War. Also a fourth leg for the stove that someone gave us. It has only three legs but it needs four legs. Grand'mère put a piece of wood as a leg so the stove is almost straight, but each time Mother uses the broom she knocks the piece of wood from under the stove and if there is a pot warming on it, it falls with a great, great noise and everything in it spills all over. It is a big mess; Mother screams and says that she does not deserve this; she also bangs the walls with her broom. This is when Just-Justine and I take Nana's hand and hide under the bed. Mother also screams at Father, even if he is not here to hear it, but she calls him a miserable son-of-a-gun and all kinds of other mean words I do not know. Mother screams a lot. Maybe that is what I got from her, the screaming, like Just-Justine got her left-handedness from Grand'mère.

Camille 1944

The telephone and the toilets

1, 2, 3, 4... No time now, scared to forget...

Sometimes we go to pee in public toilets. It is mostly because of Nana since she can never wait. The reason we go to public toilets is that when Mother wants to give a phone call, we have to go where there is a phone. You can find a telephone at the post office, but this is too far, also at the doctor's office but we cannot use his phone because he has to cure sick people with it. So we go to the café right at the end of the street. That's when we lived in Paris. (In The Village Mother never telephones).

Mother does not want to leave us alone in the house when she goes away. So we go with her. At the café we say that we want to telephone then the four of us pile up in a tiny little cabin where you first must turn a small black crank very fast and shout: "Allo, Allo Please pass me Galvany 50 19 Mademoiselle." You should always say Mademoiselle to the telephone even if it does not look like a mademoiselle. Then you wait very quietly. After that Mother starts talking louder than loud, and she cries and we cry, too. That's when Nana has got to go. It is like this when she cries.

Mother asks me to take her to the public toilets because I know where it is. You go down some stairs, and there is a door, on it, it is written "occupied" or "free". If it is free you can get in. There is a hole in the middle and two places to put your feet. Except Nana has to put both feet on the same step and kneel, because her legs are too short. Against the back wall, on the side higher is a chain that you must pull when you are finished. The

65

chain is so high I cannot reach it. I'm glad I have a good reason not to pull it because when you do, the water comes down so fast that it soaks your shoes and your stockings. It stinks in there we cannot stay too long. I always rush Nana to do her business so sometimes she just wets her panties. Just-Justine never says anything she just follows humming the song she prefers while she sucks her thumb.

You know men and boys can pee standing up against walls. They have a slot closed with buttons in front of their pants. When they want to pee they unbutton the slot and get a little tongue out and pee standing up. I know because I watched carefully a grownup man do it against a wall that had "DEFENSE D'URINER" written on it in huge black letters. "Uriner" means to pee. But he was doing it anyway. When he was finished, he bent his knees a little and shook his lower tongue so the last drop fell off.

The man looked at me looking at him and how he was doing it and winked. He said: "Getting an education, little princess?"

I wonder what men need to do when they need to poo because they do not have a slot on the back of their pants. Maybe they can also poo through the little tongue. I will ask Grand'mère. I wish I could pee standing up.

So this is why girls have dresses and boys and men wear pants, except for The Village priest and Jesus.

Camille 1944

Grand'mère disappeared

The Germans have changed France in two big toilets: one is Occupied France and the other is Free France. If you are in the occupied one, you cannot go in the free one. And if you are in the free one you cannot go in the occupied one. They put many mean soldiers with big boots and guns at the door; if you try to pass they will put you in jail. That's what Grand'mère did once with Monsieur Henri because she wanted to see some cousins who live on the other side. With the help of Monsieur Henri the Rascal who knows his way around, she passed because Monsieur Henri was a passer. A passer is a person who knows how to jump over the doors without being seen. On the way back, Monsieur Henry was not a passer anymore because the soldiers caught them. Both of them were put in jail but in separate rooms. It was the kind of special jail where they sort people out to decide if they should go to concentrated camp. The soldiers believed that Grand'mère was Jewish. She does not have black curly hair – she has white curly hair – but all the same they were very suspicious. Soldiers are like that and they have long lists to write on all the time. The people in jail had almost nothing to eat, not even rutabagas, so that Grand'mère lost a lot of kilos. Mother said she looked so dreadful that she even asked for another plate of rutabagas without complaining even once. Grand'mère said laughing that she never prayed as loudly as when she was in jail. She remembered the prayers the nuns taught her when she was a girl in school. So she had all the women recite the prayers morning, afternoon, and evening. She even asked for a priest to come and confess everyone and give the communion.

When the soldiers asked her where she had gone to school, Grand'mère gave the name of a school that was burned down during the First World War. That's right, Grand'mère has seen two wars now. So she learned a lot on how to act during wars. She knows that soldiers are thieves, it does not matter what color of uniform they wear. So she says. I'm so proud to have such a clever Grand'mère!

All the same when we were finally alone and she had finished all the rutabagas directly from the cooking pot, I asked Grand'mère how she had escaped. I wanted her to tell me how she kicked the soldiers with a stick and slapped them hard on the cheeks. She just said: "Now, girl there is something I want you to never forget:

When you think you have lost, it is never the end till the end.

Also, that everyone loves gold, so you should always carry some with you just in case."

Now I have to look for gold everywhere I can. I already have a beautiful bracelet made of gold, that's something. It took her twenty two days to walk home. I'm so happy Grand'mère is not a goner, I would miss her forever and ever.

Camille 1944

Queuing for beans

1, 2, 3, 4, ... 21,....22 , 22 makes me think of something...

In Paris, our street number was 24 rue Balagny and Madame Granet's house was number 22. Madame Granet is Mother's friend. But she is not my friend. She is very tall, with a big nose. When she hugs me I can see she has hairs inside her nose like Father. Also, she puts on perfume that she calls Mimosa and it makes me sneeze. It makes Just- Justine sneeze, too, but Just-Justine says she likes to sneeze. Nana, who does not know how to behave yet, asked her once why she has a crooked face. Mother was very upset and she locked Nana in the bedroom all by herself. But Nana does not mind, when she is put alone in the bedroom she sings or plays with MY doll and finally she falls asleep, ¬ not like me when Mother asks me to go to the room I scream and kick, it makes me very angry. All the same, this is not fair because Nana is right; Madame Granet has a crooked face. Just-Justine went under the table to suck her thumb. I hate Madame Granet and her mimosa smell and her teeth that she can pull out of her mouth. I wish the Germans would take the mimosa, too. I went under the table with Just-Justine, and I tickled her toes. It makes her giggle. Grand'mère says that the best thing to do when you do not like someone is to make as if they are not there. Just-Justine knows how to do that better than I do.

Father says I am a fast learner, but it is not true. I am the slowest learner. I get mad very fast. I am going to make a list like the Germans do and I'll write the name of all the people I do not like so I remember to kick them hard when I am bigger. Maybe that is what they do. I hope Mother, Grand'mère, and Father are not on their list. Just-Justine, Nana and I do not count because now we are baptised.

That day Madame Granet was very excited. She said the grocer on Rue de Rivoli just received a big load of dried beans, and they were selling them without tickets. Two kilos per family! Mother was running around the table, laughing. She put her shoes and her hat on, (when Mother puts a hat on, she nails it on her head with a long pin that has a pearl on one end) and called Grand'mère who was having a nap. Then she stopped. It is never good when she stops like that; it means she has an idea.

She asked Madame Granet, who was in a rush, to get the beans: "You said, it is two kilos per family?"

"Yes" said Madame Granet as she clicked her teeth in her mouth.

"Camille you come with me." Mother said, "but wait!" And she went in the bedroom where Nana was and started to open drawers very fast. In a bag she found what she was looking for — The clothes of the boy next door who died of a bad case of measles and that she had promised to go sell at the flea market. Then she pulled my dress off and made me wear a pair of pants, and a blue beret. She stuffed my hair in the beret.

"Now, you are a boy, and I am not your mother. We do not live in the same house. You understand? I will explain on the way Hurry!"

On the way, as we go as fast as we can, she says that if I do not say I am her daughter and that I came by myself because my mother is sick, then they will give me two kilos of beans extra for us. I am proud that she explains the secret to me. It is because I have the Age of Reason. She says that the reason she dressed me like a boy is because everybody knows she has three girls. Still, even in boys clothes I look like me.

Camille 1944

When we get to the store, there is a long, long line of people waiting and talking. Everyone wants the beans. We are the last on the line not for long because lots of people arrive behind us. Mother does not talk to me but she talks to other women. It takes many, many minutes. There are sixty minutes in one hour, it is fun and boring at the same time. Everyone has a large basket to put the beans in, and I have one, too. When women in front or behind me move they hit me on the face or in the back with their basket. It is not on purpose, but all the same, they forget to say "sorry". I wish I could sit, but I am afraid someone will step on me. People say that they will close the store when they are out of beans. I hope they close only after I get mine. I want Mother to be proud of me.

We got them. Four kilos of beans! So for once, Mother kissed me and is almost dancing in the street.

But you do not cook the beans right away. First, you must sort them. Beans have lots of little pebbles mixed in. So you must take a handful of them in the bags, spread it on the table and check for tiny little pebbles. If you leave the pebbles in them, somebody could break a tooth on them while you eat, especially if you eat fast because you are hungry. Just-Justine is very good at doing that; Nana not so good, so you always have to check what she does.

When the beans are sorted, Mother looks at all the pebbles we found and says, "Look at that, no shame, they make us pay for the pebbles too, the dirty rascals! No wonder the Germans did not want the beans!"

All the same because Mother is happy, we are happy too, and we dance around the table singing. We cannot eat the beans yet. First, they have to soak in water all night long. If you do not do that, you can get a big bellyache.

The next morning, it is double whammo, because we have the beans and Father is here. Father comes at night when we are sleeping. He throws little stones at the window, not so loud that other people can hear, just Mother, because he does not want the Germans to catch him. Father's real name is Benoit and Mother's name is Marcelle. But they call each other Chéri. That means they love each other. (You should put an e at the end of Chéri if Chérie is a girl or a lady, you do not say the e you just write it) Grand'mère, I'm not so sure, because when she is in a good mood she calls him "The Dreamer" and "Triple-Fool" when she is upset. Triple means three times. It is difficult because I love Grand'mère, but I super love Father too, and I do not think he is a fool. Father says he used to have scary nightmares like I have, but now he is living them in real life. Father works with trains: he has to blow them up. He is a terrorist. I heard it while I was under the table. If you do not make any noise, grownups forget you can hear what they say. To blow trains is a big job. It needs organization. I'm not sure what organization means, except one day way back I helped Nana to dress and when Mother came in the bedroom she said, "that's quite an organization!" and she laughed, so, organization is a funny way to dress, perhaps. Father is home with some friends, two big men who smile at us and at Mother.

While the beans are cooking, Mother takes us to the park; Father cannot come, because he does not like to be seen in public. He is too shy and we should not say that he is at home. Nana is a big problem; she talks too much and with everybody. So we can only play the three of us. It is fun all the same, although Mother says that public parks are nests for germs. Germs are tiny little animals, you cannot see, and they get on your hands, or your mouth, or your nose and start eating you up. That's how you get sick. I catch many of them all the time, so I get sick. The germs then jump on Just-Justine and Nana and they get sick,too.

Now when you are sick, you get very hot, sometimes your head hurts, so you stay in bed because you do not feel like playing and you just wait to die. But your mother has to call a doctor. The doctor comes and gives your mother a little piece of paper with a recipe for the name of poisons to kill the germs. Mother runs to the pharmacist to buy the things that are going to make you feel better. You wait and sometimes you cry. Sometimes you sleep. Father, when he is there, holds your hand and cries with you.

He also says: "Please, please little one, do not die!" while he holds your hand.

Then Mother tells you to open your mouth to drop the medicine in your mouth. It tastes terrible. I do not know if we do not die because of Mother's medicine or because we do not want Father to cry.

Camille 1944

The short wave radio

1, 2, 3, 4,.....35, 36,...100, 1o1...167... this time I counted much, much longer because I forgot what I wanted to talk about. There is so much to say and the beans are almost ready. We will have to share with Father and his two friends...

Oh, yes, now I remember. But I cannot speak loud about that because it is a secret. Father and his two friends have put their ears touching the radio. They are listening to the short-waves. This is where Général De Gaulle talks to the French. It is short wave because he does not say much. He cannot, because he is in England. In England, they speak English, which is funny French hard to understand. I do not know why Father is so interested in what Général De Gaulle says because it is just crazy talk, like this: "Français, Françaises, Tomorrow the rabbits will run. I repeat, tomorrow the rabbits will run."

While he talks there is a strange sound coming out of the radio. The Germans do that so we cannot hear what Général de Gaulle says, but we hear it. We are not supposed to have a short-wave radio – The Germans forbid it – but we do have one. Sometimes Father has to move the radio to a secret place because policemen come to your house to check if you have one.

The Germans hate Général De Gaulle. Général De Gaulle and short wave radios are bad words like "bum, Krauts and fuck you". Only Father and his friends are allowed to say them, because if the collaborators or the Germans hear you say them, they would send a time-bomb on your house and take your mother away for a long, long time. I do not know about Grand'mère because she has lots of tricks in her bag, she says. It is a hidden bag that she does not want me to see. I search everywhere but cannot find it.

If you do not know what a time-bomb is, it is because you are too young like Nana or Just-Justine. A time-bomb is something that airplanes spit out. It falls down and stays there for a time. Then, all of a sudden when you do not think about it anymore, it explodes, breaks all your plates and even maybe your windows or your chairs. It also leaves shrapnel that are fun to pick up and play with. But you can cut your fingers on them. Also, you should not walk bare feet outside, because you could cut your toes on them.

Behind our house, The Germans have an anti-aircraft machine-gun; they are trying to shoot the British planes while the British planes are trying to shoot the Germans behind our house. It is a very noisy kind of game; it is a silly grownup game because people can get hurt. Sometimes airplanes go down in flames, and sometimes some men get down with a parachute. Children are not supposed to watch. There is a way, I know it but I won't tell.

Camille 1944

What happens to the dead

There are goners and real dead people. Goners just disappear. There are lots of them; mostly they are goners that Mother or Grand'mère know of. But I know some, too. The real dead people are put in a black carriage pulled by two horses and driven slowly around the streets. Some of his friends follow behind the carriage. When you see the black carriage, you are supposed to stop and bend your head.

I was young then and I did not know what happens to the dead. Since we are in the Village I found out. There was the daughter of the veterinarian who died the other day. I had never met her, but since the veterinarian helped us a lot – he is the one who gave us the three legs stove and also two old mattresses – Grand'mère and Mother said, "We should go and pay our respects". Nana and Just-Justine did not need to go, since they are too young. The dead girl was asleep, all dressed up in a pretty box. The way Grand'mère was holding my hand; I knew that I shouldn't say anything and act like a well-behaved grownup. Two days after, we had to line up behind the black carriage like the one I have seen many times in Paris. We walked very slowly at the end of the line. The bells were singing their sad songs. The first person in line was the fruity priest with a long white shirt over his long black dress, but he had a different hat. That man has really a strange way to dress! There were also the priest's two sons walking behind him and dressed a little like him. You could see they were his sons. They were holding, on a chain, a little pot with smoke coming out of it. Then we arrived at a place called a cemetery. This is where you are supposed to plant the dead

Claude Beccai

people. First you make a big hole and when the black carriage arrives some men take the box out of it and put it inside the hole. Then the priest takes the smoking pot and throws some smoke over it while he says some magic words, but not in French. After that, two men with big shovels start putting earth on the box. They are planting the dead so they can grow back as trees. Some of the dead cannot grow back as trees because someone put a big stone over them. The stones have writing on them. There are also stone children with wings over the stones. Those are the ones that want to fly to heaven instead of growing into trees. When I die, I want to grow into a cherry tree and the birds, in my Camille tree, can fly to heaven and have a nice place to come back to when it is the time for cherries. I hope Grand'mère and Just-Justine grow into cherry trees, too. I do not think Mother or Father and even Nana will want to grow into trees, because they are too sad all the time. They will want to stay in heaven and watch the clouds make interesting drawings in the sky.

Grand'mère tells stories

I think the only time I can stay quiet and out of trouble is when I sit on the floor and put my head on Grand'mère's lap. I cannot do that too often because Grand'mère is busy trying to help Mother find her wits. So when she says that she needs a breather and sits on the only chair large enough for her bum, I take a breather too, with my head on her lap. This is a special time where I can ask soft questions and she answers me softly too, as if we are floating on white clouds in a blue sky. "That's what angels do." Madame Violette said to me one day, but I am sure angels do not know how to caress your hair like Grand'mère. Anyway, Grand'mère said that Madame Violette is not a good reference. Reference is a trade like the baker's wife. I'm not sure. Or maybe it is a size because I am small for my age. Maybe, it is a smell because Madame Violette does not smell good. Grand'mère says the baker's wife is a good reference and sometimes I am too. So perhaps it has to do with what you say when you speak.

I like Grand'mère's world, it is full of beautiful words and I like words, I want to know all the words. I want to become a word millionaire. There are angry words like "scram", caressing words like "you-are-my-funny-imp", loud words like "stop-that-immediately", colour words like "cerise" and expensive words like "new-shoes". Just-Justine is not so interested in words. She prefers music. She does not need to sit near Grand'mère like me; instead she sits in front of the radio and listens to music because she knows it is all there is to know.

Claude Beccai

The way to enter Grand'mère's world is easy. You sit quietly and do not move. You lend your head to be caressed and wait. After a little time, you become a Camille-Grand'mère so you can go to places you have never seen before. The Camille-Grand'mère starts humming softly. It is hard to hear at the beginning; you just know it because you can only feel it from the lap-head. It is like a soft drum. The inside head-drum beats the same way as the inside lap- drum until they melt together. They become sister drums. Then the song starts, it is a beautiful song, happy and sad at the same time. It talks about cherries, blood and smiles. Camille-Grand'mère knows it by heart.

> When we will sing of cherry picking time
> And gay nightingale, and mocking blackbird
> Will all be feasting!
> The fair ladies will have follies in their heads
> And the lovers will all feel heartsick!
>
> When we will sing of cherry picking time
> The mocking blackbird will whistle the best!
> But it is so short, the cherry picking time
>
> Where in a dream two go to pick
> Cherry earrings
>
> Cherries of love in matching red dresses
> Falling on the leaf like drops of blood
> But it is so short, the cherry picking time
> Coral pendants that we pick as we dream
> When we will sing of cherry time
>
> I will always love cherry picking time
> If you are afraid of love sickness
> Avoid fair ladies
> I who do not fear the cruel pains
> I will not live a single day without suffering

Camille 1944

When in cherry picking time
You will also feel love sickness
It is from this time
I keep in my heart an open wound
Even Lady Luck would not soothe my pain
Nor fade the memory I keep in my heart

The Grand'mère-Camille is full and the Camille- Grand'mère is not full but ready to be filled.

Camille-Grand'mère – This is a Before-The-War song.

Grand'mère-Camille – This is a Before-The-War song, a War song and an After-The-War song, as I am, and as you will be.

Camille-Grand'mère – I am a War song.

Grand'mère-Camille – If you are lucky, you will be an After-The-War song and also a Before-The-War song as everybody is in the entire world. Nobody on this Earth knows how to live without wars for long. Our only choice, if any, is to be warmongers or dead.

Camille-Grand'mère – Warmongers are war monkeys?

Grand'mère-Camille – That is another good way to call us, even if it is not fair to the gentle monkeys. Most of us – the people – think we are the masters, the most intelligent and we rule over the world. This is a dangerous disease. War is a disease.

Camille-Grand'mère – You are saying that all the soldiers have the measles?

Grand'mère-Camille – I am saying that we are all sick of a sickness much more deadly than the measles, and not only the soldiers.

A tiny number who never wear uniforms are sure survivors. They are the ones who play at war and use us as puppets in their game.

Camille-Grand'mère – Is war a fun game?

Grand'mère-Camille – It seems to be for the very rich. The rest of us poor fools believe their lies and play along. But we are always the losers. The very rich, the winners, also become even richer and more powerful playing it.

Camille-Grand'mère – Rich means that you can buy silk stockings, new leather shoes and not eat rutabagas?

Grand'mère-Camille – No, very rich means that you can buy and sell bombs, canons and yes, people. This song we sing is older than I am. I would like you to remember it, in respect of a lady who could have been my own grandmother. Her name was Louise Michel. She was put in jail many times for what she said about wars and other things. She was a very brave lady.

Camille-Grand'mère –What does brave mean?

Grand'mère-Camille – It means to do what you think is right even when it scares you.

Camille-Grand'mère – You are not brave Grand'mère because you are never scared, and I am not brave either because I do not know what is right.

Camille 1944

The shoes

The one good thing about being a grownup is that your feet do not grow anymore. So if you are careful with your shoes, if you polish them every day, glue strips of tires on the soles, watch to see if they are worn out and need replacing, then you can wear your shoes for many years.

Now if you are growing, your feet grow too, and then your mother or your father first cuts the end of your shoes, only the top not the sole, so your toes stick out. But they do not do it before you start limping really badly. There is another problem, it is that it is not only your toes that grow, and also, the whole foot becomes fatter. First, you do not tie your shoe with a lace. But then comes a time when you will have to do without shoes unless there is another child older than you and without a younger brother or sister to pass on their old shoes. I do not know why, but it is very embarrassing for Mother to let us walk barefoot in the street. She says that it is not proper. Nana, who is the youngest of us, is always the one with the worse-looking shoes.

The reason I wear these clogs completely made out of wood is because the Germans also take all the leather we have. They need it to make the big boots they wear and also the leather jackets and helmets they need to ride their motorcycles.

Mother was crying because she had no shoes to give me, so someone from a farm in the village gave her those clogs for me. They can be a lot of fun to wear even though they are quite bigger than my feet. Grand'mère filled them with old clothes to keep them stuck to my feet. When I run with them on, I make a lot of good noise and that is a fun game; also if I kick one leg way up really hard, the clog leaves my foot and jumps very high over my head. I do that only when I am alone or with Just-Justine not when Mother is watching.

Once, my clog jumped right over a fence. This was very embarrassing, because I did not dare ring the bell at the house to ask for my clog, especially because I would have to hop on one foot and I would look silly. Just-Justine had to go because she had two shoes that day.

Camille 1944

Life is full of surprises

Like Grand'mère says all the time, "Life is full of surprises". For the longest time I did not understand what she was trying to tell me, but now I know.

This girl was there when we arrived at the village, the one with the red hair – I told you about her – the one who pulled her tongue at me just as we stepped out of the train and the big important people, like the doctor and the veterinarian, and the priest, were there at the station to greet us. There was some music ,with big shiny trumpets and drums. The musicians looked like soldiers but they were not soldiers, so there was no need to be scared. They were soldiers called Fanfare, which means they do not have guns, only musical instruments. The red hair girl's name is Aline. She is the pharmacist's daughter and I talked to her. Well, she talked to me first. She is a bit taller than me and has nice shoes with a bow on top of her toes. At first I wanted to kick her, but wait until I get stronger. She told me that she does not have any brothers or sisters, so maybe when she grows out of her shoes she will give them to me. I asked her if she wanted to play tag but she did not. So we sat on a bench. We made faces at each other for fun. That made us giggle, and this is where she told me that she was taking piano lessons.

I did not know you could take piano lessons. I have seen a piano once in Paris, It looks like an armoire but when you lift its jaw, you can see all its white teeth. I did not tell her that because I did not want her to think I was stupid. So I did not say anything and just listened. She said her teacher was nice and one day if I wanted, I could go with her to listen while she took her lesson. But

Claude Beccai

I would have to be very quiet and make sure that my knees were clean, not like now after I had jumped in the mud for fun. I do not understand why your knees must be clean to play piano, but again I said nothing. The lessons are on Thursdays after school. The piano teacher is Madame Dubkoff. That's a funny name, not funny Ha-Ha, strange. She smiles at me and said that Aline told her about me. She has a bun of hair in the back of her head that she keeps up with two long pins, and she does not smell very good. She asked me if I like music and I said no, Just-Justine likes music but I like drums because you can make so much noise with drums that it can make you forget to have tantrums. The village policeman – he is called "garde-champêtre" – has a special hat and a drum, but no gun. With his drum, he goes on his bicycle to different places in the village, beats on his drum so everyone gets out of their houses then he reads from a paper with a loud voice.

I found his picture.

Maybe that is what I want to do if I grow up. So I tell Madame Dubkoff and she laughs. She says, "Well people were right about you, you really are priceless." Priceless means that you cannot be sold. That makes me very happy because I do not want to be sold ever. I belong to Mother, Father, Grand'mère, Just-Justine and Nana. When you listen to a piano lesson, you just sit, with clean knees. You can look but you cannot talk ever. I do not mind not to talk because there is so much to watch. Madame Dubkoff has a big bum, not as big as Grand'mère's, but big all the same. She sits on the same bench with Aline; it is fine since Aline's bum is small like mine. Aline's feet are dangling above the floor because her legs are too short, and her pretty shoes are waving to me. I hope Aline grows out of these shoes soon. Madame Dubkoff's feet are big fat feet all blown up, and she wears mules like Mother used to have in Paris, except Mother's feet are not puffy and her mules were nicer looking. I think Madame Dubkoff should wear slippers like Grand'mère because her feet look like Grand'mère's. Maybe she does not know about slippers. When I am allowed to talk I will tell her. When Madame Dubkoff wiggles her bum on the bench, the bench makes funny noises just like it is wishing to break, but it does not break out of respect.

Now they are all set, and Madame Dubkoff says, "Let's start with some scales."

I do not know what she means but Aline does. She starts walking her fingers very fast up and down on the piano teeth while Madame Dubkoff puts her glasses on. The song goes for a long time and I like the sound of the piano. I wish I could do the same. Then they open a book with lots of lines and some dots, and Aline reads the lines although there are no words on it. Then Madame Dubkoff looks very stern and says with a mean voice,"No, Aline, that's me, me, me, cannot you see, it is do, me,sol."

Aline says:"Sorry!" and starts again.

The lesson is finished, and I haven't moved from my chair. Madame Dubkoff turns to me, I lift my skirt a little to show that my knees are clean, but that's fine because she looks over her glasses just like Grand'mère does. When Grand'mère looks over her glasses she does not see very well. I know because I tried it on her.

Madame Dubkoff sits on the chair close to mine, puts her hands on my knees and says, "So little Camille from Paris, how would you like to learn to play piano?"

"Yes, I would, I would, I would, but I cannot"

"And why not?"

"I do not have fast fingers and I can only read letters not music."

"Listen little Camille of Paris, you must learn to trust big people like me, I am offering to teach you piano gratis pro deo. Just say "yes" if you are interested and let me do my job."

I do not know the difference between piano and piano-gratis-pro-deo, but I said yes anyway.

And she said, "Good I'll see you on Mondays at 4:00 in the afternoon. Do not be late."

Learning piano-gratis-pro-deo is not as good as learning to bang on drums, but it is still nice to learn tricky things. I want to learn everything in the world and I will be able to do fancy gymnastics with my fingers like Aline.

The first lesson is amazing. I know now where middle C is, and that the dots on the five lines have their own place on the teeth, which are not called teeth but "keys". Even so they do not look like keys. They also each make a different sound that you can sing. Sea, sea, sea. I love Madame Dubkoff even if she has swollen feet, but I would not marry her. Madame Dubkoff said I should practice between lessons. Since I do not have a piano-gratis-pro-deo at our house, Madame Dubkoff said I can come every day from 6:30 till 7:30 which is when she has supper and I can play on her piano. She would be in the kitchen. I ran and skipped all the way home. I was very happy, couldn't wait to tell Grand'mère and Just-Justine. I won't tell Nana, she is too small

Camille 1944

and wouldn't understand. To explain it all to Just-Justine, with my big toe, I drew the five lines in the dirt. It is called a "staff" and I stamped dots all over for the notes.

The next day, I could not wait for 6:30. Grand'mère said I was antsy, that means I disturbed her a lot. Madame Dubkoff had told me I did not need to ring the bell, just push the door open and go directly to the piano in the parlor.

I started to push all the keys with one finger, and you know what? Each key has a sound of its own, that makes a lot of singing sounds. Then I tried to marry two keys by pushing them at the same time with two fingers. Some are good marriages, some not. Then I stood up to push the pedals – there are three of them – and it was fun, too.

A man I do not know came in to sit on the armchair by the piano. He did not say a word, only looked at me. I did not know Madame Dubkoff had a husband. He had slippers on his feet and looked like he had not washed for a long time because his hair is glued to his skull. Father's hair is curly and jumpy like mine.

Monsieur Dubkoff must have caught a lot of lice in the Metro, because he is scratching his pants between his legs all the time and that makes him have mean eyes. I will tell Madame Dubkoff about the lice killer. That should help him. I think Madame Dubkoff sends Monsieur Dubkoff to watch me and check I do not do anything silly with her piano- gratis-pro-deo, because he comes to the parlor each time I am there and now he is itching so much that he even pulls the little tongue out of his pants and rubs it so hard that he even starts peeing and has to get his handkerchief out to wipe the pee off it. Funny that he keeps watching me with his ugly eyes while doing all that. He must be scared Madame Dubkoff will punish him if he stops watching me. I did not tell Mother or even Grand'mère about it, because they would tell me it is not good for me to see that. But I like the piano

89

sound so much. The sounds fill the parlor and my inside. Some taste like green cherries, some like rutabagas, some will even feel like they make your hair curlier.

The last day I went to play with the piano-gratis-pro-deo is the day when Monsieur Dubkoff had lost his handkerchief and he peed on Madame Dubkoff's pretty carpet. I got scared that Madame Dubkoff would think it was me who had spoiled the carpet. So I told Grand'mère. It took a long time because Grand'mère asked a lot of questions. She wanted to know everything. Then she put her hat on, and asked me to tie her shoe laces because it is hard for her to bend down. Her sciatica was acting up because of the rutabagas. She told me to come along and told Mother she was going out with me.

We walked as fast as Grand'mère can walk all the way to the bakery. The Reference, the baker's wife was there. Grand'mère asked her if she had a minute and The Reference said she was about to close shop, so if we could wait, she had all the time in the world. She gave me a flan. I like the baker's wife a lot. Then we went into her kitchen, behind the shop. You cannot see it if you only go to buy bread because it is hidden behind a curtain of beads. She served a glass of wine for herself and Grand'mère and gave me a glass of cider. I like cider.

Then she said to Grand'mère, not me,"By the way you can call me Sophie."

Grand'mère said, "You make a lot of sense to me, Sophie; this is why I am here. Do you know Madame Dubkoff by any chance?"

"Listen Granny – without a name – everyone knows everyone in this village. This is why we are so happy you and your family are here, even though it costs us some. At last someone is here we do not know – that's entertaining! (Entertaining means funny.) Now, what is it you want to know about Madame Dubkoff? Or is it more about her droopy paramour you really want to know?"

Camille 1944

I did not know that Monsieur Dubkoff's name was Droopy Paramour. That's a name I never heard before. The Baker's wife and Grand'mère had another glass of wine. I can feel that the Baker's wife is going to talk secrets to Grand'mère, because her head gets very close to Grand'mère's head. And since I am very interested and I know they are going to ask me to leave, I make like I am falling asleep. It is only half a lie because I wish I could go to bed. The cider was good and I drank it all.

"Stephane was Madame Dubkoff's husband's buddy. They both went to war, not this one the other one, the First World War. The husband did not come back, but Stephane kind of did. I mean he is not all there, if you get my drift. Now occasionally Madame Dubkoff offers piano lessons "gratis pro deo" to little girls. Somebody should have warned you. But this is a village story and you are outsiders. Sorry, if I had known I would have told you. I like little spunky Camille, keep her away from that house."

That's how I stopped learning piano-gratis-pro-deo. Grand'mère made me promise that I would not tell anyone. That meant telling Mother and Father.

Camille 1944

The story

Grand'mère said one day that maybe I should write my stories. It would keep me busy and surely people would love to read what I wrote. I do not know about that. The only person I know who reads all the time is Father. Mother says that she does not have time for frivolities; that means doing things that are not important. Washing dishes or going to the market to buy rutabagas and talking to ladies about Father and us are what mothers are supposed to do. Reading books is only for the Never-do-goods, the dreamers, the idlers. And Mother is not one of them.

All the same Mother is very proud that I can read and write. She thinks it is useful when you are out on the street so you can read all the signs, the names of the streets and the warnings: like "Butcher Shop", "Avenue de la grande Armée", "Défense d'Uriner", "Verboten" (that's a German word that means:"Do not do it" (whatever it is that you are doing), "Polizei", and "Gets-Tapo". Except the German write it "Gestapo"; it is not their fault they do not know French like we do. I do not know what Tapo is; perhaps it is a sickness like the measles, like gets-the-measles, or gets- frostbite. I asked Grand'mère and she said she did not know what I was talking about. It must be a new word from During-The-War and not from Before-The-War.

Once in Paris, Father took me to the library. It is not a nice place. There are lots of shelves with zillions of books. But you cannot touch them... Zillions means lots and lots so much that you cannot count, so zillions really do not exist... it is like Zero. You can say it, you can write it but it does not exist because it is

Claude Beccai

nothing... There is a big book in front that you can touch and where the names of the books are inscribed on it. Then you choose, and write your choice on a piece of paper and you give it to the lady standing behind a desk. After that, you wait while the lady goes and finds your book. I do not like that place. Father says that he does not like it anymore now because a lot of books are "indexed", that means that even if you want to read the book, you cannot;"Verboten".

Here is my first story. I wrote it on the back of a box of cereal Mother bought on the black market to give us muscles. Do not say "black market" aloud. Market is fine if you do not put "black" in front, then it becomes a dirty word. I do not know why, I only know that black markets are a lot more expensive than other markets.

Once there was a bird sitting on
a treetop, Its name was Tiki.

Tiki forgot how to fly, and it fell
on the sidewalk, Dead.

Tiki was stupid.

Morality: If you are a bird do
not forget how to fly.

I wrote "a morality" at the end because that is how it should be. Just like the stories a clever man from Before-The-War wrote. His name is Monsieur Jean de la Fontaine. Grand'mère does not need to read the story. She knows it by heart, That time it was the story of The Wolf and the Lamb, where the lamb gets eaten by the wolf even if it did not do anything mean to the wolf. The moral of the story is this: The strongest always wins. That means do not ever tell what you think to someone who is stronger than you, because if he thinks that your ideas are not good for him, he will be angry and maybe beat you up. It does not matter if you are right or wrong.

So, first eat all your rutabagas and wait until you are at least as tall as Madame Geneviève. I will never wish to be a lamb, but I have to let Nana know about that.

The other day, Madame Rose said to Mother about Nana, "She is adorable, a real little lamb!"

It scared me for Nana, because she will be eaten up when she meets a wolf and she does not know it.

I read my story to Just-Justine and Nana.

Nana cried and said she did not want to listen to anymore stories, because she would be real scared to find a dead Tiki on the sidewalk.

Just-Justine kept humming while sucking on her thumb. That's normal because Just-Justine is too smart to say what she thinks.

Grand'mère said that I was a dangerous thinker. Sometimes it is very difficult to understand Grand'mère especially when she makes strange little clicking sound with her lips.

Father cried like Nana because Father does not want anybody to die except Nazis.

But Mother was too busy to read it or even listen to it.

Camille 1944

Doing the N

I have tried several times to show Just-Justine how to do the N, but she does not like doing it the way I do it. It is too bad because it would be more fun to do it together.

If you are in a bad mood, and you need to pout, the best thing to do is to sit with your back against the wall with your feet close to your bum, hold your legs and put your head on your knees. You look like a big N. It is easy to do. You can start by screaming for a while. Then you hum very loud to show everybody that you do not like what is happening right now. Your Mother might tell you to stop, just make as if you did not hear and that you do not care anymore. If you get bored you can wiggle your toes for some fun, but do not forget to keep humming.

The humming goes in your belly and your head, then it goes to all over your body until you are nothing but the humming that makes you feel like you are a bubble that floats.

You are not anymore in the village, not in the house with the rats that eat the food Mother kept for supper, not where Mother's friends think you are an ugly pest, not seven years old, you are no age. Your outside eyes are closed. No Boches, no collaborators, no resisters, no scary things like time bombs, no Nana to protect. What I like is that you start looking with your inside eyes. First, you only see little color dots that change in a picture, but you can think of something and the picture comes on. Or you do not think of anything and new pretty pictures come. It is better than when you dream because you can choose.

Claude Beccai

If you are lucky you fall asleep in the shape of an N; if you are not lucky some idiot shakes you because it is time to go to school or do something that is not fun.

Camille 1944

Photo Album

Mother

Father

Nana, Justine, Camille

Grand'mère

Camille 1944

On fire

It is not that I do not want to talk about it... something happened that I do not understand and I do not remember all of it... even so I know it happened. Grand'mère had gone to an errant when it happened, so she wants me to tell her and I do not know how to start. But I even know less how it finished.

Grand'mère said,"I want you to look at me all the time when you tell me and I also want you to remember that I love you no matter what. Start with the beginning."

I always look at Grand'mère's eyes when I speak with her, except when I put my head on her lap. I like looking at her eyes because they talk to me without words. The beginning is easy. After we arrived at the village, we have been going to that school where we can eat at lunch and we are supposed to eat a lot so we won't be hungry when we get back home. It is a school with two classes: One has the little kids and the other has big kids. Normally the three of us should have gone to the little kids 'class, but somebody decided that only Just-Justine and Nana would go to the small kids' class and I would go to the big girls' class. It is because I can read well and multiply of course. But I am the smallest in the class. For lunch, we all meet in the same room that is not called a dining room but a refectory. So Nana, Just-Justine and I stay together at the big girls table. That is because Mother says I am supposed to look after my sisters no matter what. It is easy for Just-Justine she never talks, but very difficult with Nana. Nana is noisy, she talks nonsense, she laughs, she cries, she pees in her pants when she laughs or cries and tells everyone about it because she has not reached the Age of Reason like I did. I think it will take her a long time to do that. Just-Justine has reached the Age of Wisdom like Grand'mère that's why she does not get in trouble.

We were sitting at the table, with both hands crossed when the big tureen arrived. The biggest girl at the table took it. That girl, I do not know her name but she is bigger than Mother so she is the chief of the tureen. There is lentils soup in the tureen and it smells really good but we have to wait politely for our turn to get served by the big girl.

Grand'mère's eyes are quiet, they are listening.

The big girl passes the tureen in front of Nana's face and asks her if she wants soup. The big girl is smiling and Nana says a loud yes. The big girl laughs but does not give her any. Nana is waiting politely. The big girl serves some soup to other girls then she asks Nana again if she wants some. Nana says Yes. The big girl laughs again and serves some more soup but not to Nana, I do not understand why. I hope that fatso would ask me, if I want some soup. I would say no even if it is not true.

Grand'mère's eyes are getting smaller; this is what happens when she gets upset.

Nana's face looks very sad, I wish I could console her but I do not dare.

It is so difficult to tell the story that I cannot breathe right and I am stiff all over, I do not know how to cry, I never cry I only scream.

Now Fatso with a big grin on her stupid face asks Nana again, and this is when I feel fire all over me and I do not think anymore. I jump on the table, upset the tureen on Fatso's face and all over her dress and her boobs, I grab the water pitcher, break it, Fatso is up against the wall and I am going to kill her, I am a Nazi even if I am not dressed in black.

I do not know how I end up in Mother's bed with big knots inside my belly maybe I flew. I know something really scary happened. That's all.

Grand'mère holds me tight, and says it is all over now, little one. I love you. But I shiver and it takes a long time before I can breathe again quietly. It hurts a lot inside for a long time when you are on fire.

The next day I do not tell anyone but I go to school to finish killing the big girl but she is not here. I never see her again. Maybe she went to concentrated camp to burn the goners in the big oven. Nobody talks about my yesterday's fire, in the refectory we are served first when the tureen arrives and the teacher is very nice to me, maybe because she is scared. I am scared too; I did not know there was another Camille inside me. That other Camille does not know anything about the Age of Reason and I cannot talk to her she is hiding most of the time.

Camille 1944

My God!

A lot of grownups have a god. That's easy to know because they keep saying: "Oh, my God!" for all kinds of reasons. When a bomb explodes and breaks the windows:"Oh, my God", when the milk spills over the cooking pot:"Oh, my God", when you sneeze in the bowl of soup:"Oh, my God", the thing to say if you are grownup is: "Oh my god!" or "Sweet Jesus" when something happens you did not expect. I tried it but it does not work for me and it is because I do not have a god.

Since I go to Church on Sundays for the mass, I have seen where they put God. It is in a small box on top of the table with a table cloth that is called a tabernacle. Only the village priest can open the box when he wears the long white shirt over his black dress and one of his sons helps him. When the priest opens the cabinet everybody bend their head, I do too, but I look all the same. Then it takes a long time for the priest to wash the dishes even so his son helps him and there is only a cup to wash. If Mother saw that, she would not be impressed; she would say:"It is just like men!". Mother thinks men are slow thinkers when it comes to doing the cleaning. I think she is right, Father is a man and he is super slow.

I still do not know what God looks like, so I decided to make him look like a ball. I took some bread and went to hide inside a cupboard to roll the bread until it looked round, I had to spit a bit on the bread to make it easier to roll, also if you put some boogers in it, it sticks much better. To get the good boogers you need to go far inside your nose because the easy ones, almost on the outside, are too dry to use.

I kept my head bent all the time, which is what you do when you touch God. That was easy because there is not much room in the cupboard. If you go hide in a cupboard you need to kneel and bend your head, like in church, so it is a good place to make a God because gods like churches and fruity priests. I stole Grand'mère's shoe box to make a nice tabernacle and I put some dandelion flowers in the box too, to make my God happy.

I had to find a name for my God, I did not want to call it Jesus because I saw a picture of Jesus in the church and my God does not look at all like him. Jesus has long hair and he looks very sad even when he drinks wine. My God looks like a bomb. I am going to call it Person. That's a nice name and nobody knows Person except me now.

Even though I kept the secret, and I gave Person flowers every day, a rat came to eat it the other day. It made me sad.

Camille 1944

Black the rabbit

I will never eat a rabbit ever, ever, ever.

A friend of Father gave us a baby rabbit when we were still in Paris. The baby rabbit was so cute and I loved it right away. That's "LOVE AT FIRST SIGHT" like Grand'mère says. Father made a cage for it and put it outside in the yard. The rabbit has a soft white fur and red eyes. Just-Justine, Nana and I, we all three kissed it.

Grand'mère said we should give it a name, and since it was a friend we should call it by an English name in honor of General de Gaulle who is now in England to fight the Germans in Germany and who is sending us messages every day on the short waves radio. I did not tell Grand'mère that General de Gaulle did not make much sense to me but I wanted to be polite for once. So Grand'mère who is the oldest and has good ideas said that Black is a good English word for the rabbit. Madame Juliette who learned English in school a long time ago said that black is not the colour of the rabbit; it is white, so it should be called White. But Grand'mère likes to have the last word, even with Madame Juliette who knows a lot since she went to school longer than Grand'mère; Grand'mère said that is was a good thing because it would be a good Resister's name for the rabbit. I like Grand'mère all the way to the sky.

Black is growing fast because we give him lots of grass. You do not need food tickets for grass. Germans do not eat grass. Black is a tricky resister. One day, he disappeared and we looked for him all over. You know what? We found a tunnel that he had dug. Father poured water in the tunnel so Black would not like it, because he does not know how to swim, but Black is a clever rabbit and he dug all the way to the neighbor's yard. Madame Boudasse gave it back to us. That was very decent of her! So Mother invited her for supper sometime. Madame Boudasse also gave us dandelion leaves for Black since now she knows about Black even so it was to be a secret that we had a resister living with us.

If you do not want to hear what I am going to tell Cesar, I understand. I will not tell Just-Justine either. Cesar is the only one that I can tell, because I believe we understand each other, and I am going to marry him anyway.

It was the day that Grand'mère was talking to Mother like she was telling secrets. She was wearing her funny eyes, the eyes that said:"You know what I mean." And Mother was making moves with her head so that only Grand'mère would understand. When they do that, I make as if I am busy playing with something as if I do not care, but I listen with both my ears, because it is important and I want to know. Grand'mère said to mother:"Keep the little ones inside!" Then she left with a big knife that she put in her pocket. As soon as Mother was not looking I followed Grand'mère and hid behind the lilac.

Grand'mère went to Black's cage she grab him by his fur and twisted his head. Black made a funny little noise. Then Grand'mère cut his throat with the big knife and cut it so that a lot of blood runs down his fur. Then she took his fur off, after that she put a pot under him opened his belly and took his heart out. Grand'mère's hands were full of blood. I had put my hands in my mouth so I wouldn't scream, because I knew she did not

Camille 1944

want me to see what she did. I swear I will never trust her again. Grand'mère went back in, but I stayed behind the lilac a long time because I could not move, I was shaking too much.

When I went back in, Mother and Grand'mère were busy in the kitchen and I went to hide under the table.

At night Madame Boudasse came for supper; all the grownups were happy, even Mother was smiling while eating Black but I did not want even to taste it.

I think that now I know what the Germans do to the goners.

Camille 1944

The exodus

They called it The Exodus, I do not know that word. It happened a long time ago, I was small then. I think I was going to be four. Father was not with us, he had gone to fight the Germans with the photo of all of us in his pocket. We were in Paris but we lived quite far from Grand'mère's apartment. Grand'mère came for a visit but she said we were all going to live at her place, because we were all done for and it would be better if we were all together if we were going to die.

Mother and Grand'mère got the pram out and filled the bottom of it with lots of baby cereals, then they put Nana who could not walk well yet, she could not talk either, and then they put Just-Justine in the pram too, I think she was two. Then they said that I could walk. I did not mind because normally when we went to Grand'mère we took the metro or the bus. I did not know what we were going to do with the pram because you cannot put the pram in a bus and even less in the metro.

There were a lot of people outside, but it was not a feast, nobody was talking. There were also a lot of dirty soldiers who spoke French; they told Mother and Grand'mère that the Germans were right behind us. One put me on his shoulders because I couldn't walk anymore. There were no buses and no metro, all the stores were closed which is strange because the soldiers said that Paris was an open city. I do not remember too much, I think I fell asleep on the soldier's shoulders and when we finally arrived at Grand'mère's place I could not go up the stairs, my cousin came down to carry me up.

Upstairs, Grand'mère started running all over the place and opening all the drawers, and asked Aunt Mimi to help opening more cupboards. Then, they climbed on chairs and put little things behind the mirrors. After that she asked me and my big cousins to sit on the carpet to tell us that we should never, ever say "Boches" and to never, ever look at the mirrors if the German soldiers came to see us. She said that we had to be well behaved, and she looked at me when she said that. That day, I did not like Grand'mère at all because she was not being nice.

Mother said that she had to go buy some milk. Since Grand'mère looked so angry, I wanted to go with Mother to buy the milk. I screamed until she said I could go with her even if she had mean eyes when she said that. She made me promise that I would not make a sound. Even then I could keep a promise.

Mother told me to hold on to her skirt because she needed to keep her hands free. The street looked funny. There was a bunch of soldiers walking right in the middle of it because there were no cars. The soldiers walked all the same way throwing one leg way up and then the other while they were singing a nice song that I did not know. Mother and I we were on the sidewalk but Mother stopped because she wanted to cross the street. The soldier in front of all the other soldiers saw us, he lifted his arm, that made all the other soldiers stop, but they kept singing and beating the street with their boots. Then the soldier in front showed us with his arm that we could cross. So we did. Then the soldiers started to walk again kicking their legs way up.

On the other side of the street Mother knocked really loudly at the door of the milk store that was closed, nobody answered, so we went to another street and banged on the door of many closed stores. Mother was crying so I cried too, even louder. Then a window opened and a man said:"you better run home, Lady" and Mother said:"Not before I get milk for my babies" and the man gave her some milk and we went back to Grand'mère with the milk. After that I do not remember anymore.

Camille 1944

Cesar my fiancé

We are not the only refugees in the village. When we were in the trains to get here we stopped and slept in a town. There were other people who also had travelled in trains. The soldiers said we had to be sorted.

Some men, who looked like soldiers, took us first to a big room where they gave us each a metal bowl with soup in it. At first I did not want to eat out of the metal bowl because I told Mother I was not a dog and she was not one either. But Mother asked me to try the soup anyway and showed me that she was eating too. I tried it and I felt it was good because I was very hungry. Then some other men came and removed the tables and gave Mother a card with our names on it and a number, Mother was not supposed to lose it. After that it was time to sleep. We each had a cot and they gave each of us a bag to get into. They called it a sleeping bag. I went in the bag, but it scared me. Someone could come, shake the bag until I get to the bottom and he would make a knot on top, and then dump the bag in a hole with me in it. Mother tried to put me in her bag with her but the bag was too small for both of us. I was scared. The next morning we were put into a smaller train with a lot of other children, also from Paris. There were some other grownups, from Paris too. These people were the teachers for the children in the train. One woman had a big belly because she had a baby in it. Grand'mère has a big belly too, but she does not have a baby in it.

All the children from Paris are boys. When we arrived in the village, the teachers stayed with the village teacher at the public school and the boys stayed on farms.

Claude Beccai

The woman teacher, the one without the big belly, says she likes me, her name is Mademoiselle Ducrocq. She says I am entertaining. So when she goes to visit the farms where the boys are she takes me along, and I am supposed to tell her stories. It is sometimes boring because she asks lots of questions. I am not sure if it is because she is daft or if she wants to know if I know what I am talking about, anyway it does not matter, I like telling stories and fibbing makes me giggle. One day I will invent a great big lie that will go as high as the clouds, then it will burst like a bomb, and the shrapnel will fall on a thousand and one people, go under their shirts and tickle them so much that they will roll on the floor just laughing, the Germans, the French, and General de Gaulle and Maréchal Petain, even Hitler the maniac will laugh.

We go from farm to farm. We visit five farms each time.

When we arrive at the farm, Mademoiselle Ducrocq goes inside the house and I wait outside. Someone brings me a glass of milk, and I go visit the hens, I stay away from big animals because they scare me. But hens are fine. It is fun to throw some grain to them. There is one farm I like a lot, this is where Robert lives.

Robert is the Parisian boy; he is twelve and a half. I know he is a resister because he told me so. Robert knows a lot, he told me he has been around. He also told me that he has a tail and he showed it to me. In the back, boys and men do not have a tail, their bums look just like girls'. He told me to never let another boy or man show me their tail until I was at least fifteen or sixteen when I would have good size boobs. When I told him I would rather have a tail, he said that it did not matter because I had balls just like his mother had. I did not know what it meant but I did not ask. I did not want him to think I was stupid. That day, Robert came to say hello and told me that, as usual, Mademoiselle Ducrocq was in the barn, having her jollies with the farmer's brother. He said it was alright because at least it was not with a fucking Kraut, sometimes he talks with strange words; I do not tell, I cannot anyway because I do not understand a lot of the words. I will ask Grand'mère for the meaning, I cannot ask Father because he will tell me to go ask Mother and Mother will just say:"Who told you that? I do not want you to talk to him anymore." To have the jollies means to like to be amused, it is true Mademoiselle Ducrocq likes to be amused.

We went for a walk because Robert wanted to show me something. As we walked he said that I was young, but smart enough to enroll in the resistance. I was very proud. I had, first, to go through the ceremony. Ceremony is like a mass but without a priest and it is not done in a church, Robert said. We had to dress up. We went inside the chicken coop where Robert keeps his treasures in a suitcase. The one he brought from Paris. He got a beret, a gun and a dried up red flower. We went behind the chicken coop and he taught me a song. This was not hard because I already knew it but I am not allowed to sing it ever, even if it is Father who taught me. It is the Franc-tireur song that the Germans do not like. Then we marched around the chicken coop throwing one leg at a time way up, Robert also checked if I could resist torture without saying a word, he pinched me really hard, I kept my mouth shut. Robert then told me to salute him. He said that I was a good recruit and now I had to obey his orders because he was the corporal and I deserved to meet the captain and we went to the apple orchard. That is where the captain stays. I told him I had to pee first but he said we did not have time for foolishness but since I was a girl, I could go fast in the ditch and he would stay on guard.

Cesar is the captain. He does not speak quite like us. He told me he is Spanish, he cannot say Camille the right way, he cannot say Robert the right way either. I do not know who Franco is, but Cesar hates him, so I hate him too, because I am in love with Cesar and if he is not a fascist I will marry him if I turn to be a lady. Cesar is a brave resister and he wants to kill Hitler, the maniac, with his own hands. He has a little sister my age, but he does not see her anymore because she is in Spain and he cannot write to her, because the Nazis would know where he is and they would find him and take him to forced labor in Germany. Forced labor is where you make bombs for the soldiers even if you do not like making bombs. Cesar prefers to stay at the farm and work there because he can eat cherries and eggs. I told him that in Paris, they were throwing bombs away, and that broke many houses and trains, so we had to go to shelters when the bombs fell down from the airplanes. The airplanes were British airplanes, sometimes they were American airplanes. You had to be very careful of airplanes because even if they mean well, they did not know where to throw their bombs. He said the Germans are scared now and to be very careful of scared people. People are dangerous when they are scared. I did not know that. It means I am dangerous because I am scared a lot.

The reason I love Cesar is because he talks to me the same way he would talk to grownups and he shook my hand. That makes me very proud. Also he told me that it is not important if you swallow the cherry pits, that it is even very good for you tripes. The tripes is what you have in your belly and end in your ass hole, that's what he called the hole you poo from. Ass is not a word I will say aloud in front of Mother. I will not tell also how Cesar talks because she will forbid me to go see Cesar. She says I will have to turn into a proper lady whether I want it or not. I do not want it. I want to marry Cesar because he talks to me as if I am a real person. The other time I met Cesar, I saw him three times in all, Robert was not there because he had to go to do his homework that he had not done and Mademoiselle Ducrocq was mad at him. So, I went by myself in the orchard and he was up on a ladder helping the trees to grow up. When he was finished he came down and we sat on the grass. We talked. Then he looked at me really seriously he took my chin in his hand and he said that he could see I was a very clever girl and that was not good at all. He said men do not like clever girls because clever girls scare them, and women do not like clever girls either because clever girls could guess their secrets. So the best thing for me was to learn to look silly. Then we played at looking silly. That was a lot of fun.

The last time I saw Cesar, he was very busy, he said he had no time to talk to us; he had something very important, dangerous and secret to do. After that, no one saw him anymore. I think he is a goner, Robert thinks so too. Robert thinks that Franco found out where he was hiding and caught him.

Camille 1944

How to keep warm

In the village, we have a wood stove, to keep warm, but also to cook. In Paris we had a coal stove to keep warm, but not to cook. You needed tickets to buy coal, tickets and money. Children like Just-Justine, Nana and me got more tickets than grownups but old people did not get any tickets. So even if they had money, they could not get coal for their stove and they were always cold.

Mother invited a lot of old people to come to our house every day to keep warm. They sat in front of the stove, and talked and knitted, or made balls of wool from old clothes that were full of holes or were too small to wear. First you un-knitted the old sweaters or the socks, then you made the yarn into a neat bunch, and you washed it and dried it. Once it was all dried, you had to make it into a ball, before you could knit it into something nice and warm to wear. You need knitting needles to knit, some are thick and some are thinner. It all depends on what you want to make.

All the old people are not grandmothers; that is why they come to our house. They try to help Mother because Mother is nice to them. All these old people do not look as nice as Grand'Mère, and two or three of them are really stupid. Madame Miami does not have any teeth in her mouth or anywhere else, Madame Granet wears her teeth in her pocket most of the time because she says that they hurt a lot in her mouth. Mother does not know how to do that trick; I mean to put your teeth in your pocket, which is because she is still too young. I think Madame Granet is at least 35 years old. She told me that she is 85, but I think it is a lie, because I do not think she can count that far, she cannot read either, she always asks me to read for her. It is boring stuff but I do it anyway, because Mother said if you are clever, it is to help people who are not. Madame De Bur knits all the time, but her sister talks really loud and sometimes forget to put on her dress and Madame De Bur must run after her with the dress, but her sister screams and says that the Germans are coming to take her to the concentrated camps, even when it is not true at all. There are also the Ludwig's, they used to be singers in a theater but they cannot sing anymore because the Germans do not like the way they sing even though they are not French, Monsieur Ludwig is a Baritone and Madame Ludwig is a Soprano Coloratura. I think the Germans are right; I do not like their singing either. All the same, it is not right to not give them food tickets or coal tickets just because their singing is awful. That is why I stay quiet politely when they sing. Monsieur and Madame Ludwig do not know anything except singing. They do not even know about knitting. So they bring us books that are useful to light a fire but it makes them both cry when we tear the pages off the books they bring. I do not know if they cry because of the smoke or if they really, really loved their books and are sad to see them burn. They do not cry like children, they cry like old people, no sound, only tears rolling down their crumply cheeks. They use a lacy handkerchief to wipe their tears.

 Madame Granet' work is to feed Nana. I think she likes doing that because she likes tasting Nana's food, to check if it is not too hot. You know what makes Nana really laugh? It is when Madame Granet blows on the food. Because with her teeth in her pocket, Madame Granet's lips are all soft and when she blows air out of her mouth the lips make the same sound as wind in the trees. The lips clap at each other making a funny noise like little farts. Nana thinks Madame Granet makes that on purpose but I know better because I am so much bigger. She blows like that many times, she also eats almost Nana's entire bowl maybe it is because she thinks Nana is too fat. When I told Mother about Madame Granet's eating, Mother told me to be quiet, that she

Camille 1944

always made something extra for Madame Granet, because she was hungry and that made her ashamed, so we never should mention it, ever, ever, ever... When Mother says ever three times, it means you better obey or else... Then Mother winked at me that means we share a secret. I like that.

There is also Monsieur Octave who comes but not every day. When he comes Mother gives him a kiss on the cheek. He likes that, it makes him get all red in the face. Monsieur Octave has an axe. So when we do not have any more coal for the stove, Mother looks around and decides which piece of furniture we can burn, we burned so far the nightstands, the cornice on top of the buffet, two armchairs. Monsieur Octave takes them and breaks them with his axe so it fits in the stove. Monsieur Octave is really strong even if he has a wooden leg. He cannot put the leg in the fire because then he could not walk anymore.

Sometimes when we have burnt all the coal, mother calls the doctor and say one of us is sick, then the doctor has to come. When he arrives, he asks Mother who is sick in here, and Mother says:"The stove", the doctor smiles and writes a prescription for the stove. 50 kilos of coal. Then Mother goes to the coal merchant, who delivers a bag of coal on his back, we light the stove again and sing a nice song when it is warm. Everybody is happy. Mother does not want to burn all the furniture because she says she does not know how long the war will be. Some people say that the Germans are finished, but you cannot believe what everyone is saying. Beware of what you hear! In the village it is a different story altogether, because we do not use coal to warm up, we use wood.

Camille 1944

The war at home

Sometimes Mother turns into a German. She does not call Father Cheri anymore. It is because she gets very mad at Father and she wishes she would have a bomb to throw at his face. So she is just German without a bomb but she makes a lot of noise all the same, and she says bad mean words to him. Some words I know, some I do not. She says bastard, that means a big bread that you only get with ticket, or on the black market behind the baker's store, sometimes she calls him a stupid genitor I do not know what that means but I think it is a machine you can put in a motorcycle. Then she bangs on a pot with the lid, many times and that makes an awful noise. Mother is grownup angry.

When Mother is angry like that, I am so scared I close my eye real hard but not so that I cannot see and I put my hands on my ears real tight but not too tight, Just-Justine sucks her thumb really hard with the thumb all inside her mouth. When she does that it means she is scared too, because when she is not scared she only sucks half her thumb. Nana sings and talks non-stop to her doll.

Father is stronger than Mother, but Mother is a better German. Mother takes the broom and bangs on the wall so hard it looks like she is going to break it, but it only makes dirt marks. Then she lifts the broom as if she is going to hit Father's head, but usually she changes her mind maybe because once she did hit him and then Father had a bump on his head that hurt a lot, and she had to fix him. Then she runs up to him, because she wants to hit Father with her fists, but Father holds her fists in his big hands. Mother keeps saying mean words.

Claude Beccai

This is when I think that Mother is going to leave us alone and never come back because she is fed up with all of us. That's what she says anyway. Father takes a cup or a plate or something and throws it on the floor. It breaks. Mother is angrier than angry; she looks at Father in the eyes takes two or three plates from the buffet and breaks them too. We used to have 24 plates of the same sort and six with different flowers on them. Grand'mère gave them to Mother one day to be nice. But now we have only 3 left of the nicest ones and two of the uglier ones. They were plates from Before-The-War. They did the same to the glasses AND TO THE CUPS. You know what they both say to Grand'mère after? That WE break the plates. But I told the truth to Grand'mère, as a secret. She did not punish them at all. She smiled and said that we should keep it as a secret. NOT FAIR! Then Father takes something else, one day he took the alarm clock and threw it through the window. The window was opened so the pane did not break, but the clock did.

When something bigger than plates breaks, this is the end of the war. Father gets the broom and starts sweeping. Mother stops screaming; sit at the table and cries. Father picks up the broken plates, puts his arms on her back and says: "Cherie" nicely. Mother says: "Do not you CHERI me!" but not so mean and she cries even more. Father sits beside her and cries too. This is when we can come and kiss them, but not right away.

I wish it would be the same with the real Germans, we the French would give them something big to break like the Eiffel Tower, which would make everybody sad, and it would be the end of the bomb war and we would all like each other again.

Camille 1944

The ration tickets

If you do not know what ration tickets are it is because you are too young, you are dead or you are a goner. You do not need ration tickets in the village, so maybe that's it; you are from the village since ever. So I will explain it to you just one time, I know all there is to know about them.

Just-Justine, Nana, Mother and I we go every month to the city hall to get our tickets. Mother has to show that she is French, and has a card that says so written on it. It also says that she has three children and their age. She will get two times tickets for Nana and Just-Justine who are J1 because they are less than five years old, then one time for me, because I am J2, that means I am more than six, and she will get one time for her, she is a grownup but not an old person, if she were old like Grand'mère or Madame Granet she would get less tickets. Tickets tell you how much you are allowed to eat.

When we get to the city hall, Mother goes to wait at the end of a long queue of people, Nana, Just-Justine and I we sit on a bench that runs all around the big, big room. We have fun gliding along the bench on our bums or we watch the ladies who sit in front of a desk behind the counter. We wait until Mother gets the tickets.

The tickets come in lots of different colors to buy different things to eat, to wear and to put in your stove. The bread tickets are brown because you cannot find white bread anyway, the fruits and vegetables tickets are pink because of the color of carrots even if you cannot find carrots, The Germans like to eat all our

Claude Beccai

carrots and leave us the rutabagas and the Jerusalem artichokes or the turnips that make Grand'mère and Madame Granet fart really loud. The milk tickets are yellow, they are only for children. I do not know the colors of the other stuff. Father does not get tickets because he is illegal; Maréchal Petain said so, since Father does not want to go to work in Germany. Sugar is only for children too. Grownups drink chicory instead of coffee and put saccharine in it. These are called Ersatz, it means not true. There is no butter because the cows are now Germans, so we get margarine instead. Margarine is also Ersatz butter. There are other kinds of tickets that you do not get at the City Hall; you buy them from rascals like Monsieur Henri. You do not have to give money for the tickets at the City Hall but Monsieur Henri sells his tickets. Monsieur Henri is a good tickets merchant, because his tickets look a lot like the ones you get from the City Hall, but they are false tickets and you must not talk about it. It is a secret. You have to wait to make sure there are a lot of people in the store and so the merchant is too busy to look at the tickets real well, and you must mix them with good tickets from the City Hall, if the merchant sees the Monsieur Henri tickets you must look very surprised, and say you do not know where they come from even when you know they are from Monsieur Henri, because Monsieur Henri will get really mad at you and will never sell you tickets anymore. Mother and Grand'mère are good liars, and I am learning very fast, but they still do not trust me too much. Father is a worse tickets liar than I am so Mother does not give him any false tickets. Anyway Mother says that Father always looks guilty even so he almost never is, I think it is because he has a mustache or because he does not have a nice pleat on his pant legs.

    Now if you listened to me carefully you know all about ration tickets, but what you do not know is that even with all these different color tickets everybody is still hungry. Even Mother one day fainted because she had not eaten for three days and she had been carrying Nana up the street, and she said she was floating in her dress. I do not know how one can float in a dress, but she can, she said so.

Ration Tickets ©Collection CHRD/ Ville de Lyon

Camille 1944

The markets

I know of three kinds of market.

There is the regular market where there is very little to buy and what there is to buy you must give tickets and money to get it. It is never enough says Mother. It makes her very sad and sometimes angry like all the other mothers she knows. When the mothers meet at the market, they say:"How are you, my poor Dear?" and they talk about the price of rutabagas, they roll their eyes, then they talk about us the children, who give them a lot of worries, they also talk about their husbands who give them more worries. And us the children, we wait politely behind her and make faces at each other to have a bit of fun, because we hate it when mothers talk together. When we are really fed up, we grab our mother's skirt and pull her away, or we have a fight between each other, or we jump in a puddle and get really dirty so we must be rushed home to change. We do not do it on purpose, it just happens. Some mothers slap their children real hard, but Mother never slaps us. She just gets sadder.

There is the black market. That is very tricky even for me. In the black market you have to be a grownup. Because you must know how to talk with your eyes and sometimes with your hands, and all the while you talk loud with your mouth. But your mouth does not say the same thing as your eyes.

Also you must keep your eyes seeing behind your back. I do not know how to do that yet, but I am learning. For example I am good at spotting if someone I do not know is listening to what mother and the merchant are saying. If I see a curious man or woman I pull not too hard on Mother's skirt. For example if you find an egg you would want, but you do not have the egg ticket with you. The egg with ticket would cost two francs but without ticket it costs ten francs and you must know what kind of sign to make with your fingers and understand the eye talk of the merchant. It is very complicated, but when you finally get the egg in your basket you must feel very happy and not forget to watch that somebody you do not know is not following you. You could go to jail, unless you give the egg to the person who is following you. I do not know why this is called the black market, I never saw anything black sold on the black market except the finger nails of the merchants, and sometimes his teeth but these are not for sale.

Finally there is the Flea market but there are no fleas there. It is called the Flea market to fool the dummies and maybe to scare them. You go to the flea market to get some money, so you can buy things on the black market. First you look in your drawers and all your hiding places at home to see what you could sell. Maybe some old clothes or shoes you do not need anymore because they were shoes from a goner, and he won't need the shoes anymore because he is going to be cooked in the big German oven. Maybe it is a ring that your husband gave you Before-The-War, and you do not need it anymore because your fingers became smaller because you did not eat enough rutabagas. Sometimes it is a painting that you found very pretty Before-The-War but now you prefer to buy a pair of shoes with it. There are many things you can find at the flea market. Mother does not buy at the flea market, she sells for herself and for other people who give her a little bit of what she gets for the dress or

Camille 1944

whatever she sells. The people she sells for are too scared to go themselves. Maybe it is because they think there are fleas there, but they are wrong.

There are some very dangerous people at the flea market. You know they are dangerous because they have good shoes with leather soles, a nice coat and a hat. They are the Maréchal Pétain's men. These are meaner than the German because they speak French and they understand what you say. They are more rascally than Monsieur Henri, Grand'mère told me because Monsieur Henri is living from hand to mouth and he is not vicious, but these men are filling their pockets on the poor starving folks like us. That is what Grand'mère says, and she is right most of the time. (But, that's not true what she just said. I saw Monsieur Henri eat at our house. He uses a fork, and he winks at Mother) So four eyes are better than two, especially two eyes of a clever little girl, who is going to save her mother from the rascals. There are also a lot of nice, clever and funny people at the flea market. Some sing funny tunes in Parisian slang, that only Parisians can understand, they let us know that a rascal is near when they change the way the song goes, this is when you go and put something in their hats to thank them. There are a lot of German soldiers who come to the flea market because they like to be in Paris, it is like a holiday to them. Everybody is laughing at the flea market, except the Maréchal Pétain's rascals. It is fun when the war becomes a big, big joke for a while. One day a nice man gave me an orange. I had never seen one before. Mother had shown me a picture of one, and she had told me it was like a little sun. She was right. There were a lot of people around me watching me peel it and laughing. It was also fun to share the orange with so many happy people. I only ate a little piece; even some German soldiers came looking and laughed. I wish everybody would laugh like this all the time. When you laugh a true belly laugh, you love everybody and everybody loves you.

Camille 1944

The provisioning

When Mother fainted because she had not eaten enough rutabagas, the doctor came and pricked her arm with a needle and made her eat a bowl of soup. Then he said to her, that she should also eat and not give everything she had to us, because if she disappeared we would disappear too. That scared me, and I think it scared her too. So she had a long talk with Madame De Bur. They talked for a long, long time, so long that I think I fell asleep and I did not hear everything.

Mother lived in Normandy when she was a child, so she knows a lot about it, like I know a lot about Paris. Also Mother, during her child war, lived sometimes in a farm and she had learned about cows. Mother was ten when her war started; she lived in Dieppe at the time. Dieppe is a city like Paris but much, much smaller, and it has a sea. A sea is a place with lots of water, I have never seen a sea, only on a map that Father showed me once, and it is very blue. Father was also born near a sea, but not the same one. Mother moved to a farm when she was 13 and that is when she learned all about how to make butter and talk to farmers. It means that if Mother can find the farmers she will also find the butter. I will go with her because I want to help her.

Madame De Bur knitted a very nice blue hood with a scarf attached that will keep Mother's head and neck warm, because it is cold in Normandy. At the flea market, Mother also found a pair of boots with soles made out of wood that make Mother's feet look fat and funny. The boots are a little bit too big but it does not matter because Madame De Bur also knitted a beautiful pair of thick socks and cut a pair of inside soles out of one of Father's old felt hat. Mother will be snug as a bug to walk in cow's poo. It is mostly cow's poo in Normandy because it is the countryside.

    I had to throw a great, super big tantrum to be allowed to go to Normandy with Mother. It made Madame De Bur scared of looking after me while Mother would be gone. Just-Justine and Nana are not a problem because they are adorable, but I am a pest and I want everybody to know it. I am six after all, not a baby anymore and I can read really well. Madame De Bur is so happy that she will not have to look after me while Mother is gone, that she made me a pretty pink backpack out of her crazy sister's old dress.

    Very early, it is still dark when we leave the house. Madame De Bur said "Merde" thirteen times to Mother. That's what you say for good luck if you are French. You should never ever say "Good Luck" because it will turn into bad luck. Luck is when you find a good bread ticket someone lost on the side walk, or if you trip but you do not fall. There are not too many people in the street, we go into the metro and we get off at the train station, Gare du Nord.

    There is a lot of noise, a lot of policemen and soldiers, many different trains, a huge clock, and voices to tell you where to go. I am holding Mother real tight, I am afraid to lose her because I do not think I could find her again, but she could not find me either, I feel very small, and I have never taken a train before, only when I was a baby and we went to Marseilles but I do not remember, Nana and even Just-Justine were not born yet.

    Some policemen ask Mother for the card that shows her French name, they also want to know where we are going even if it is written on our train tickets. She says that we are going to see a cousin who is sick, they ask for his name. She says Cousin Basil. I know she is lying but I do not say anything. She made me promise to not talk. I do not talk and I make sure I remember the name she said. Cousin Basil, Cousin Basil, Cousin Basil.

Camille 1944

There are so many people in the train that not everybody can sit. I was supposed to have a seat by Mother but I had to sit on her lap to give my seat to a very old man who could not stand too long on his old legs. It is a much longer trip than it should normally take because the train has to stop many times because of bombs. When you need to go to the toilets, the people who sit in it must leave. They did not want to leave just because of me and I did not want to pee in front of them, so Mother had to say that she had to go to and I went with her. It is difficult to find your seat back.

In Dieppe, we went to sleep in the house of a lady that Grand'mère used to know. She is nice. She let us sleep on her floor in the attic because she said times are hard. The next morning we went in a smaller train but not for as long as in the first big train, we got out at a very small train station. Then we walked, and walked, and walked. The countryside is not so pretty, and there are not many houses, but there are a lot of cows in the fields. On each side of the road there are deep ditches and you can see pretty violets growing at the bottom. There was a plane on fire in the sky, and a man jumped out of the plane in a parachute. Mother and I we had to hide in a ditch, Mother told me not to make a sound and I did not. Some German soldiers with guns came in the field to kill the parachutist but they did not kill him, they just forced him to go with them. We got out of the ditch only when Mother was sure that they were all gone. Then we went to a house. It was a farmhouse.

There was a big woman in the house and after a little bit, a man too. The woman gave me a great big glass of milk. I said thank you nicely because I had promised Mother I would be super polite. I did not understand the people very well, they do not speak French the same way as in Paris, but Mother understands completely. I think I fell asleep at the table because I forgot what happened after the glass of milk at that first farm, but we went to other farms and each time I got a glass of milk and sometimes some bread and sometimes some cider. I also got a bowl of really good soup.

Mother was asking all the people we saw, what they needed. They said shirts and pants. Mother filled her bags with apples, some butter, some cream and green beans. Then we took the train back to Dieppe and Grand'mère's friend's attic. Her name is Madame Bellocq, and she gave us some herrings, we had to eat the fish right away, we could not put the herrings in the bags because they would smell too much, but we gave some green beans to Madame Bellocq. You must be very careful when you eat herrings because there are lots of small bones in herrings so you could choke on them, and this is not very nice.

The Dieppe train station is much smaller than the Paris train station, but you must be very careful because it is easier for the policemen to see you, also the police want to look into your bags if they think there is food in your bags. Because that is not a good thing. We have lots of forbidden things in our bags, the cream and the butter and even the beans. The beans are not so bad, so Mother put them on top of the bags. We have some apples too, apples are forbidden too, but not so much. It is butter and meat that are very dangerous. What the police can do is take your butter, your milk, and even take you to jail. Mother told me that I must look sick. That is easy because I feel very sleepy. The train is smoking and whistling and the wheels under are making a lot of noise, and we left almost on the time it said we would leave. There are not as many people as there was in the train from Paris. But the people do not talk they look scared. I think Mother is scared too, she put the bags under the bench where we sit and I put my head on Mother's lap.

I am too tired to feel scared. A lady, who sits across from us, tells Mother that the train will stop in the middle of the countryside after half an hour we travel, and that is when the

Camille 1944

food police will get in to check all the bags. She said she knows because she travels in that train every week. I think Mother likes that lady, because they talk a lot together but I do not care.

The lady was right, not too long after the train had left the Dieppe station, the train stopped, and some men climbed in the car we are sitting in, I think they look mean, but I do not care. When they come to where we sit, they ask Mother to get up and show her bags, then the lady from across us said:"Do not you see that child is very sick?" then the man said:"What is wrong with her?" Mother said:"I think she has the scarlet fever." Then the men went to ask other people for their bags because they do not want to get the scarlet fever. The lady winked at Mother, I do not know if Mother winked back at her. I think the lady and Mother have a secret together. I slept all the time in the train.

When we arrive in The Paris train station, there were many, many people, and policemen, but nobody asked us any question. We were lucky. We took the metro, and the bus. But we had to climb a long hill to get to our house; it was night so there was nobody in the street because of the curfew. I felt very strange. It was as if everything was turning around me, I could not walk straight even when I tried and Mother had to wait for me because she had to carry all her bags and couldn't carry me too. It took a long, long time to get home. I wished I could just sleep on the street but Mother did not want me to lie down even if I thought that it was the best idea. I vomited all Madame Bellocq's herring.

I was sick a long time after that, I stayed in bed for many days. The doctor said that I did not catch the scarlet fever, I had caught the exhaustion, and it is a disease that makes you want to sleep all the time. Anyway I never wanted to go to Normandy anymore, so when Mother went, I stayed with Madame De Bur and Just-Justine and Nana. Mother got some very ugly shirts and pants for the Normandy farmers.

Camille 1944

Nana, the accident

I did count to 50 before I talk but not aloud because I think that what I heard from under the table is a secret and Mother would not like me to repeat it, so I will only say it like a secret and no one will hear it.

The table is big and has a long table cloth that goes down to almost as far as the floor. I like to go under the table because it is like the shelter where we must go during the alerts, bombs cannot fall on your head and grownups do not tell you what to do because they are busy listening to the airplanes. Nana likes the under the table game too, this is where she talks to her doll, but I do not listen. Just-Justine likes it also; this is where she sucks her thumb and where nobody wants to put mustard on it. Grownups say that if you put mustard on the thumb you suck, you will not suck it anymore. But Just-Justine likes to suck her thumb; I think that is how she can get into thinking. When I am under the table I can hear grownups talking, because if you do not make noises they forget you are there and they tell each other things that they do not want you to know. When you listen to grownups, sometimes you can learn things.

One day, Grand'mère was visiting and drinking hot water with Mother. Grand'mère was talking about us and said that she knew it was difficult to find food to feed us. Mother was saying that she tried as hard as she could but life was not fair. Grand'mère said that Mother had no choice, and that we were three beautiful angels. Then Mother said:"you know very well I did not chose to have three children, and that Nana was an accident! It would have been too risky to get rid of it."

Claude Beccai

I do not know if Grand'mère knew, but I did not know that Nana was an accident. I know what an accident is, it is when you spill your glass of water because you were not careful enough, or when you trip on a stone outside. It means you do not do it on purpose but I did not know a person could be an accident. Nana is very small and lots of grownups do not think she is a person, but I think she is a person. Now she is a person accident! I look at Nana and I do not see a difference with me except she is smaller.

Nana plays with dolls, I do not.

Nana laughs a lot, I do not.

Nana does not know how to have tantrums, I do.

Nana cannot count to 1001, I can

Nana sleeps a lot, I do not.

Nana came out of Mother's belly, I did too.

Maybe, all these things that Nana cannot do are the reasons she is an accident, so I am going to teach her and she will not be an accident. Except sometimes an accident is a good thing, like when Mother found a 10 francs bill under the bed when she was dusting, or when she met Monsieur Henri by accident in the metro, they made friends and he sold her false tickets to buy four delicious slices of ham at the black market.

There are some happy accidents and some sad accidents. I want Nana to be a happy accident, I will tell Just-Justine and maybe Grand'mère. I think Nana does not care.

Winter 1942

I forgot if I told you about the winter 42. That is how Mother and all the grownups call it. It was a snow cold winter. That's what everybody says and I say it too. I was five then, Nana was two and Just-Justine was three.

One morning we woke up and there was a lot of snow on the ground outside. Snow is very cold, so you need to have a fire in the heater, but to make a fire you need coal, and we burned the last coal we had the night before even though there was no snow on the ground last night. Mother told us we had to stay in bed until she found a solution. Mother always tries to find solutions. Father is not good at finding solutions. Grand'mère is very good too, but she was not there. Sometimes I think I am good too, but nobody likes my solutions. I found a solution for Nana, Just-Justine and me; we just hid under the blankets and played at tickling our toes. That is always fun.

When Mother had found the solution, she took the blanket off our heads and started to dress us up. I do not have a coat, because I grew out of it. It is Just-Justine who got it. So she wrapped me in a shawl. A shawl has three sides, a long one and two shorter ones. What you do is put the long side against your neck, then take the ends of the other two sides, cross them over your belly and make a knot in the back. The problem is that like that you cannot move your arms anymore, because if you do then you get cold on your sides and Mother is angry at you. She says:"I told you not to wiggle!"

Mother also cut some of the moleskin cloth that covers the kitchen table and wrapped it up around Just-Justine's shoes and my shoes and tied it up with a cord she found in the drawer, but not on Nana's feet because she decided she was going to carry her inside her own coat. Nana thought the snow was lard and she said she did not want to walk on lard. So we got out of the house and stayed very close to Mother. Father was away trying to blow trains up or something to make the Germans angry.

We slowly walked through the snow, the sound of our feet on the snow was very amusing, it cracked and our funny boots were wonderful, Just-Justine and I we loved them. Mother not so much. Mother said we were going to a warm place because she did not want us to catch pneumonia. Pneumonia is like the measles but you spit more, you need more medicine and even sometimes you need to get some needles. A boy from up the street, I did not know him, but he died of pneumonia and they had to make him take a walk in the black carriage with the two horses. He was lucky, I wish I could die and be allowed in the black carriage in the wooden box. Mother got very angry with me and told me to stop talking nonsense. Like Grand'mère says, Mother and I we are not seeing eye to eye. Maybe it is a joke, because Grand'mère smiles when she says that.

Mother's solution was to go to a movie theatre, because it is warm in there. It was the first time I had been at a movie theatre, and it is very interesting. There is a lady in a box with windows, that is where you must say how many tickets you want and you give your money. Mother only had to pay for two tickets because she said she was going to keep Nana on her knees and Just-Justine and I we would fit on one seat easily. Mother said it is just for us to keep warm for a few hours and the lady in the box said:" know what you mean." A movie theatre is like a church. You are not supposed to talk loud and there are rows of seats tucked to the floor, but it is dark and there are no windows, just a big red curtain in front. Then the red curtain opens all by itself, everything becomes dark for a little while, and a white curtain

Camille 1944

starts to light up. This is when you see big, big people move on the white curtain and they talk very loud. First you see German soldiers and bombs falling and the man they call Hitler with his mustache, and he raises his arm straight in front of him, everybody watching raise their arms too, and sing. Not in the movie theatre, only on the white curtain. I do not understand what is happening and I cannot talk to Just-Justine because she is asleep with her thumb in her mouth. Nana is sleeping too, on Mother's lap. I want to see everything and I hold Mother's hand so she does not get too afraid.

After the Germans are gone from the white curtain, the theatre lights are turned on and the red curtain is on. That's the intermission, we can go to the toilets, when we come back from the toilets there is a woman singing on the stage in front of the red curtain, then she goes behind the red curtain, and the white curtain comes back. Some big people speak French, but I do not understand what they are saying. The movie is called "*The Daughter of the Wellman*" I think the wellman is the man with the big teeth. He is angry, I do not know why people would watch that. It is a movie for grownups. Mother likes it. I do not, but I cannot sleep, there is too much noise.

Camille 1944

The savages

The day we arrived at The Village, after the Fanfare had played a song or two at the train station, we marched with the Fanfare to the market place, but there was no market. We were the market. We were three families left over because the school boys and their teachers were in a different group on the other side of the market place. The three families had to make a line. The Fanfare went away, and the villagers made another line in front of our family line looking at us, as if we were apples from the black market that they wanted to buy or not. Mother said we had to look smart and well behaved. I was holding tight to Mother's hand because I did not want to be bought, but even if I felt like it, I did not dare to have a tantrum to shame her.

A big man with a blue, white and red scarf across his belly told us that he liked us and that all the people here wanted to invite us for a nice meal in their house. Each village family was going to pick one of the refugee children for a meal, and every day after that until the end of the war. For the first night we were going to sleep at a hotel, until they found a house for us.

Grand'mère was not a child but she was chosen first, I think it is because she has white hair and hurting feet; she went with the baker's wife, that is what she said she was. Nana and her doll were picked by the hair dresser, I think it is because she has very curly hair. Somebody came to me but I hid in Mother's skirt so they picked Just-Justine. I hoped Just-Justine would say no, but she did not because Mother told her she had to be reasonable for two. That meant I wasn't reasonable. Another person came for me and this time I cried loudly and I did not want to let go of

Mother's skirt even when Mother was ashamed of me. Mother told me that I should have the age of reason, but I did not care. The people who wanted me got scared and left.

Mother and I, we went to the hotel room to wait for Nana, Just-Justine and Grand'mère. There are two real beds with bed sheets and blankets in the hotel room, there is also a big basin with a large pitcher full of water in it and a toilet so Mother told me to undress and helped me to clean, then she cleaned herself, her face and under her arms and her bum. Somebody knocked on the door, we were lucky because we were all dressed up again and presentable. It was a nice lady who brought us a piece of chicken with some round green things that Mother called green peas. Those are good. Mother said that I used to like them Before-The-War, but I did not remember. The woman said she did not know we were two, she thought that Mother was alone because she would have brought more food. So we ate with our fingers in the same plate. Mother always says that only savages do that. That is too bad, because it is fun. I love being a savage.

Camille 1944

The castle

After we had fixed our new house, found out how we were going to sleep, eat and wash, Mother sat down with Grand'mère to decide on important decisions. Grand'mère took the only chair with something to rest your back and mother took one of the stools (there are two good ones and a wobbly one). Mother said that since we do not have a gas range we needed to keep a fire going all the time even when it is not cold outside. The fire does not need to go full blast all the time but it needs to be easy to make alive fast. They sent me outside to see if we had wood to feed the fire. I came back and I said we had 32 big pieces of wood near the door. Grand'mère said the logs would last us for a while, she said ten days. She said we go on an expedition in the village to discover and talk to people. She called it orientation. The village policeman lives across the street from us.

Grand'mère went to talk to him but first she polished her shoes by spitting on them and rubbed the spit, she comb her hair. She has only two dresses because we could not bring too many things in the train. The dress was crumpled and we do not have an iron to press it back to beautiful, but Mother and Grand'mère wet their hands and ironed it back to nice. That will do.

When Grand'mère came back from across the street, there was another table discussion with Mother. The village policeman is on the side of the law. The law is no poaching on the land of the castle of the baron. The baron is out of the country but the baroness is in with her son. She is a fine lady. The good thing is the castle is only two kilometers from the village and it is surrounded by a big piece of land with lots of trees growing on it. So if we can borrow a wheel barrow it would be easy as pie to get wood for the stove. Except, we do not know if it is poaching or not. My head swims with all this new ideas. To be in a village is a new kind of game.

At night, Grand'mère said that she had to rest her old bones, Mother said that she would lie with her and we three sat at the end of the bed to listen to Grand'mère. Nana fell asleep, Just-Justine is leaning her head on my shoulder, she lets me ask questions, that is how she never gets in trouble because she does not talk.

I asked Grand'mère what a baron is.

She closed her eyes, and said nothing for a long time. That means she is going to talk for a long time once she opens her mouth and that I must listen. Then she opens only one eye and her mouth a little bit. That means she is not sure I will understand. Mother says to grand'mère:"I know what you are thinking and I do not think it is a good thing..."

Now Grand'mère takes her voice of story teller that I love. And it starts with Once. I have to learn the story by heart so I can tell Nana when she wakes up, and maybe explain the parts that Just-Justine does not understand.

"Once,... No, first I wonder if you remember in a park we were in and tried to find four leaves clover in a patch full of clover, and how long it took to find one."

This will help when I talk about the nobles. There are as rare among us people as four leaves clover in a clover field. The others, the us, are the commoners. The nobles are not especially beautiful or clever; the only thing that makes them special is that both their father and mother were nobles. Nobles have lived among us for perhaps 4,000 years and they have ruled us for that many years. Not only in France but in all the countries we know. What made the Nobles strong is that they were the ones who

Camille 1944

had the guns and the cannons. That allowed them to keep the things they stole, to use anyone they wanted, or kill them if they complained.

The nobles enjoyed wars, it was their favorite game. Not too many of them died in the wars they played; their soldiers, who had no choice to enroll or not because they were owned by the warring nobles and had to obey, died.

Now, not so long ago, in my grandmother's grandmother's grandmother's grandmother's time, us the commoners got pretty fed up with this kind of arrangement and we cut the head of the biggest noble, the king, his crown fell off with his head. We also cut the head of his queen, her crown fell off too. As we were shortening them we sang and danced The Carmagnole, I will teach you that song sometime. We also cut the head of many other nobles, not all of them because a lot of them got scared and ran away to England or Germany or elsewhere. Silly of us, we got drunk and cut the heads of other people, we shouldn't have.

The nobles are all cousins, and they got scared that the commoners of their own country would get the idea from us and start killing them too. So, from there on, wars continued almost nonstop. The problem is we have been used to obey for so many years that we think we need to have someone to tell us what to do, and also to blame if things go wrong. The thing we learned is that if we are not happy with the chief we choose, we can cut his head off and replace him by another one, maybe worse."

Grand'mère stopped talking; she fell asleep with her nice dress on. Also she never told me what a baron is. I do not think it was a good idea to promise I would remember. That night we all slept on the same bed.

The morning after, we borrowed a wheel barrow from the blacksmith and we went on exploration. Not too far away we found a forest, and started gathering dead wood. That was fun. We almost filled the wheel barrow. A lady came by and talked to Grand'mère. The lady had big boots and pants like the Nazis in

Claude Beccai

the Metro, but she was not dressed in black, she had a black bowl on her head and no gun but a whip in one hand and on the other hand she held the leash of the horse who followed her. All the same, I took Just-Justine and Nana with me to hide behind a tree. Grand'mère called me but I did not want to come out from behind the tree and I held tight to Nana. Grand'mère talked some more with the tricky Nazi, and when finally Grand'mère was alone we came out of behind the tree. The wheel barrow was full just enough that we could still roll it, we started back to our new house. A boy-man met us, he smiled and said he could help us push the wheel barrow and he put Nana on top of the dead wood. Then he gave us turns on top of the wheel barrow. I know the man was a boy because he did not have the little black dots on his cheeks,  even so he talked like a man and he was tall like a man, also he laughed like a boy and he was a super wheel barrow pusher. His name is Adelhard and he is the son of the lady with the horse. The lady with the horse is the baroness who lives in the castle. She is a four leaves clover not a Nazi.

The next day, Adelhard came to our new house with a donkey and a cart full of logs just short enough to fit inside our new stove. We are the luckiest.

Camille 1944

Father comes back

Mother is sick, she cannot get out of bed. Grand'mère wrote to Father because we are too much for her to care for. I said I would look after the family but she does not trust me even though I know how to give Mother the medicine the pharmacist gave us. I can do it nicely in a clean glass with really fresh water, and I can comb Mother's hair without pulling too hard. We manage together but Mother's legs are wobbly, so she cannot really stand up, and the medicine is not good enough. I tried the Jesus trick of laying of hands to cure the sick and the dead, but it does not work on Mother. Mother's belly is round like a balloon and she called me Darling. That's what worries me a lot, because Mother never calls me Darling, she must be dreaming with her eyes open. Grand'mère makes strange clicking sounds with her mouth, that too, is not good. It means there is something in her head that wants to come out, but she is swallowing it.

Monsieur Duprez, the principal of the public school came tonight he brought us a pot of soup and told us that Father will be here soon. That makes me happy even though I know that Father is not as good as Mother in finding solutions, but he is very good at holding your hand.

Father arrived in the middle of the night while we were asleep. He will sleep on Nana and Just-Justine's bed, they will sleep on cushions like I do, until we get organized. Mother is happier, but her legs are still very wobbly so she cannot walk.

She can only pee in bed while Grand'mère is holding a frying pan under her bum, then she goes to empty the frying pan in the toilets outside.

It looks like Father and Monsieur Duprez know each other and that is not normal because they never met before, but they talk like they are friends. Monsieur Duprez says we must look like a normal family. So Father is the bread winner. I did not know that there was a bread game that you could win, but Grand'mère said that it only means that you do something somebody wants done and he gives you money for doing it then you can buy bread with the money. I explained it all to Just-Justine and Nana. Nana said that she hoped that Father would soon be a shoe winner because her shoe will be dead soon and that is true.

Monsieur Duprez found a bread winner doing for Father. It is to break large stones into smaller ones to make a road in the countryside so that farmers could bring their cattle to the market. The earning was not big but it would do and the people will lend the hammer. Monsieur Duprez said it was essential we blend. Blending is when you make café au lait. You pour milk into your coffee, which is not coffee but roasted chicory and it blends into a new color. Like what I do now with my clogs, I blend into a farm girl instead of a refugee girl, except all I need is to have dirty toe nails, but that is easy to do.

Lots to learn. Fun.

Now Mother has decided to make another sister. She is tiny and I love her but she does not have any teeth and all she can do is suck on Mother's breast. I want to call her Apricot, because her face and all her body is red but Mother has number one choice so we will call her Juliette, that's better than Mimosa.

Grand'mère has gone to live in another house, because Father has first choice to share the bed with Mother. Juliette is in a basket.

Camille 1944

Playing school

Sometimes we play school. I am the school mistress of course because I am the biggest. Nana and her doll, Just-Justine and two logs are the pupils, logs are good as pupils, you can stand them up, except they fall a lot.

First, you must check if the pupils finger nails are clean. You cannot learn anything with dirty finger nails, you just play pretend with the logs, they do not care. Then you say:

> "Children, be quiet now, when the teacher is talking. Today, we are going to talk about riches, carrots, peaches and electricity."

You say "we" even if you are the only one talking because teachers must be polite.

"Madame Grand'mère said the other day: "This village is rich!", and do you know why she said that? Of course not, because you are too small, but I will explain it to you. There will be a test after the lesson. If you do well, you will be able to go and play at recess, if not, you will have to do 'tours de cour' and wear the dunce cap."

'Tours de cour' is when you are not allowed to play at recess, you are only allowed to walk by yourself around the playground and the other pupils in the middle say "boo, hoo, hoo" to you. There are two reasons you have to do 'tours de cour', one is because you are dumb, the other reason is because you are sassy or impertinent. If you are dumb, you do 20 'tours de cour' if you are sassy, you do 40. That takes all recess time. Sassy is like black market, it costs more.

In the middle of the playground, the ones who boo are not all the same. The louder ones are the ones who are so glad they were not picked to do the 'tours de cour' and they want to show the teacher that they are very obedient; there are some who do it because it is something to do and they want to show they understand the game, even if they do not. There are also the ones who do not boo because they like you or because they are busy doing something else. Just-Justine and Nana are like that.

But-I-digress! This word is not a swear word, you can say it aloud, Grand'mère says it all the time, That's what she says when she starts telling us that she is going to do a mushroom omelet for supper, then she sits down, puts her elbow on the table and her fist against her cheek and tells us about the beautiful set of dishes she used to have before-the-war. Her eyes go up looking at the ceiling, she has a nice smile and then she shakes herself and says: "but-I-digress." and she gets up.

"Let's continue. I know we haven't studied electricity so much lately. Let me remind you that if you had electricity you could listen to the radio and even the short wave with General de Gaulle. That's a fact. Fact is a small word easy to spell and extremely important. It tells you what is what. Like, you are a girl, that's a fact. You are not in Paris, that's a fact too. Now I will explain electricity to you and you will understand.

Mimosa, stand up! And Cauliflower, stop leaning on Mimosa, you make her fall.

As I was saying, first you take a big tall tree, not just one. Many. Then, you cut all the branches from the trees, the leaves too, and the bark, and you do not call them trees anymore, you call them poles.

Camille 1944

You plant the poles real deep in the earth on the sidewalk; you tie black ropes at the top of the poles. The ropes go all the way to the next pole as if the poles are holding hands, and on and on. Now if your house is not the house of riffraff, smaller ropes tie the pole to your house, this is how you get electricity that the poles suck from the earth. Some trees suck peaches or cherries from the earth, poles suck electricity. Carrots do not come from trees.

Now before we go to recess we are going to sing the Hymn to Rascal Maréchal Pétain. All together now : WORK – FAMILY – FATHERLAND" Always remember that Rascal Maréchal Pétain is our savior and the other rascal Laval, his helper, is always here to help you.

Nana is asleep again but Just-Justine is nodding, she is a good pupil.

Camille 1944

The village is happy

The ones in the village that have electricity and the short waves know that the Allies have landed in Normandy fighting the Germans for the butter and the camembert. That is why the church bells ring a long happy song, so loud that you have to shout if you want to be heard. Everybody is happy and every man in the village wants to wear the resistance insignia, the little blue, white and red ribbon that they put on their jacket to show how brave they are. I have one too, Robert, my corporal, made it for me. Except he did not have the good color pencil to draw it, so mine is dark gray, white and light gray and it is on paper because we did not have anything better to make it. Robert tore a page of his notebook to make it. Also, now you can say Boches aloud. People smile at you when you say it. Maréchal Pétain is not happy because he wanted to be the one to save France from the hoodlums but the Allies think the hoodlums are not the same ones. Also some men are carrying rifles on their shoulder even in front of the village policeman. The village policeman makes as if he does not see it. Before, no one was allowed to show a gun, if you had one, you had to hide it behind the chicken coop or else the rascals from Vichy would take you to jail and you would be a goner.

I turned eight, I am very proud; also, my front teeth are starting to show a little. Just-Justine is six and she does not stutter as much, so she is changing her name to Justine most of the time. Mother has stopped forcing her to use her good right hand, that's what the doctor said she should do. Nana is five now. Juliette is nothing.

Claude Beccai

It is summer, no school, I'm happy too. Mother is singing to Juliette and Monsieur Duprez, the school principal is helping Father to break stones somewhere outside the village, when they come back they both sit at the table and talk seriously about things. Monsieur Duprez says to beware of the Sunday resisters, Father laughs. Then they go for a little while to listen to the short waves in the basement of the school. Father comes back with some soup for us all except Juliette. Juliette does not eat soup.

In the village, I learn many more new beautiful words for vegetables: cauliflower, green peas, eggplant, mushrooms, those you must search for in the forest after the rain. Also, if you put a bone in the soup when it cooks, the soup will taste better.

Camille 1944

The Germans are kaput but on their way

Some bad, bad things happened. People are talking in low voices difficult to hear. They say that in a village not far from where we are the Germans made a big oven in a church, then, put all the village people in it to cook them. The village name is Oradour sur Glane. Also, in a city like Paris but much smaller, they call it Tulle, it is not far from where we are, the Nazis killed many men. They call it the Tulle massacre. I do not know what a massacre is, but it is not a good thing because grownups make a strange face when they say it. It is also a word you can say aloud, more so, when you say it, grownups think, you are clever but not sassy.

The Nazis are madder than mad because they are losers and it looks like Général de Gaulle is winning with his short waves. Now the village people think what happened in Oradour-sur-Glane is what is going to happen to everybody here because some German soldiers are on the road with their tanks. We are all in the school yard and we have to wait until someone makes a decision. I stay close to the boy's toilets because it is a good place to know what is happening and I see many men throwing their resistance insignia in the toilets, for safety. Nobody wants to be a resister any more.

Mothers call all the children into a classroom. The biggest and loudest mother said we are going on a trip, in the night. The first one of us who talks is going to get whacked, and the other ones who talk after that will be left on the side of the road all alone to fight the Germans and their tanks. There is no need to be afraid Monsieur-The-Mayor has a good plan..

The small children and their mothers will walk on the middle of the path, the bigger children will help carry the food we take with us, the men will walk in front of the line and also behind, they will have their hunting guns, please use the bathrooms before we leave. Mothers make sure your babies do not cry.

This is a new thing for me, I am very excited, I can hear my heart pounding in my head. All of us are going to sneak in front of the Germans. That is a super good plan! We are playing hide and seek and the Germans are not going to find us.

At first we walk to the end of the village, but not for long, then we are in the woods, between trees. Our feet make a noise or the dead leaves and the small twigs that fell from the trees, the birds are not chirping, but there is a huge round moon up in the sky, and that moon is smiling at me. Just me! I did not know such a moon could be so beautiful.

That is the greatest day or night in my life! And this is thanks to the Germans and their tanks.

As we arrived in front of the castle, we could all sit, but not the men with their guns, we could drink some milk right out of the bottles; we spilled some because many of us did not know how to drink from a bottle. Then we fell asleep. I did too, with the moon right above the castle roof while the grownups are sharing secrets.

We wake up because Father and Monsieur Duprez have arrived to tell us that the Germans are gone from the village after they got some food from empty houses. They were starving so they fed them and we can go back home without fear. Even if we can talk loud now, because we are not playing hide and seek with

Camille 1944

the Germans, everybody whispers. That is because of the moon, you cannot talk loud when the moon is shining so bright. That was the best night of my entire life!

Camille 1944

War is dead

Grand'mère is not with us anymore, she went back to Paris to organize. Grand'mère is a good organizer, but there is a woman who just arrived in the village, she is not a woman, she is Marne Carmean and I love her to the moon and back because she has a true smile. Not the smile that says:"You know what I mean." Or "I'll get you soon" It is not a smile that comes from her head, it comes from inside her belly and makes you feel warm. She is the only one I will talk to now that it happened because I am dead inside but not for her. She saw what happened when I turned into a resister and a Nazi all at once, she also saw Father turn into a collaborator and she cried. I would like to console her but I cannot, I am not strong enough. I only want to be planted in the cemetery with a big stone on top of me so I won't grow back as a cherry tree and no angel to fly to the sky, I want it dark.

Mother is in bed with Juliette sucking at her breast, Father is back from breaking stones and he is lying by Mother because breaking stones breaks his back. I sit on the stool by the bed because I like watching Mother and Juliette. Just-Justine and Nana are outside playing. Mother asks me to go watch over my sisters, particularly Nana, so I go outside on the street. Nana is trying to jump rope, she is not very good at it yet. She keeps missing the rope when it reaches her feet. So she waits until the rope is on the ground and then she steps over it, and tries again. You must keep quiet when someone is learning; you cannot talk when you think.

Across the street, there is a new family that moved in from Marseille, I do not know if they are refugees. There is one boy who is taller than me, I think he is nine or ten, he does not talk, he does not smile but he comes out of his house as soon as he sees us out. One day, I went to him to ask if he wanted to play hopscotch, he did not answer he just went right back to his house. I think he is afraid of me even though he is much bigger. He has three older sisters who call him their baby brother. He also has a grandmother who does not talk like a Parisian. She talks with a Marseille accent but not to us. She never talks to us because we are riffraff. Do not know what riffraff are? Riffraff are what you sell at the flea market, so it is good stuff even if it is not new. The villagers like that family from Marseille. Sundays, the whole family goes to church together and takes the nicer seats, the ones with the cushions, right in front, close to god in its tabernacle. That god must prefer the Marseille accent to the Parisian accent. I saw the doctor and the veterinarian kiss the hand of the grand'mère right after church.

The baker's wife says that this family has upturned noses, but I looked and I couldn't see any difference in their noses.

I started talking again because Marne Carmean with the good smile did not know what to say, or how to say it, she only can listen. Grownups do not know how to explain, they use big words, and close their eyes when they think things are too difficult for you. They have too much in their heads and not much left on their skin. This is why I never want to become a grownup.

This is what Marne Carmean saw.

I am sitting outside, on the doorstep of our house, the boy comes out and watches Nana jumping, he looks sneaky. He comes to Nana and pushes her hard enough to make her fall and he laughs. Nana is just five and much smaller than the boy. She gets up, Nana does not understand mean. I do. Nana does not understand angry. I do. I do not move because Mother and Grand'mère told me I have to control my anger. That's what you do when you have the age of reason. Nana starts jumping again, and again the boy pushes her hard and laughs. Nana falls and gets up, her mouth makes as if she going to cry but does not. Now I know this boy is a Nazi and Nana is a poor bastard. The boy comes close to Nana with a smile. This is when I jump and ram my head against his belly as hard as I can. The boy falls and starts screaming. His three big sisters come out of the house, yelling that I am a pest. I grab Nana's rope and start turning and turning with the rope so they cannot get close to me. I hit one of them. The one I hit stays there crying.. The other two run inside their house screaming. It is war! I won! I am a resister in the middle of the street! I am on fire all over!

The hand-kissed grandmother comes out. I cannot use the rope for her. She bend down to scold me, she says I am a tramp. Her head is near me, I see her pink skull between her white hair. My hand jumps all by itself and I pull a big clump of her hair so hard that the hair stays in my fist. By now, there are lots of people on the street; the village policeman is there too. I am a resister and also a Nazi because I am going to throw this grandmother in an oven and laugh a big mean laugh. I am guilty.

The noise on the street got Father, with his broken back, out. I feel happy because he is to defend me because he is a resister too. He looks at everyone, and then comes to me , I raise my arms to jump to him. Instead, he slaps me really hard, then, he pushes my head into a window, my head breaks the window and he keeps pounding on me. Now I know Father can turn into a collaborator, he collaborates with the villagers because he is afraid they will throw us out. He wishes to kill me and I hope he does because I will not say sorry.

War is a lie. I will not talk ever again.

Camille 1944

Comments

Le temps des Cerises

Quand nous chanterons le temps des cerises
Le gai rossignol et merle moqueur
Seront tous en fête
Les belles auront la folie en tête
Et les amoureux du soleil au cœur

Quand nous chanterons le temps des cerises
Sifflera bien mieux le merle moqueur
Mais il est bien court le temps des cerises
Où l'on s'en va deux cueillir en rêvant
Des pendantsd'oreille...
Cerises d'amour aux robes vermeilles
Tombant sous la feuille en gouttes de sang...
Mais il est bien court le temps des cerises
Pendants de corail qu'on cueille en rêvant !

Quand vous en serez au temps des cerises
Si vous avez peur des chagrins d'amour
Évitez les belles!
Moi qui ne crains pas les peines cruelles
Je ne vivrai pas sans souffrir un jour...

Quand vous en serez au temps des cerises
Vous aurez aussi des chagrins (peines) d'amour!
J'aimerai toujours le temps des cerises

C'est de ce temps-là que je garde au cœur
Une plaie ouverte!
Et Dame Fortune, en m'étant offerte

Ne pourra jamais calmer (fermer) ma douleur...
J'aimerai toujours le temps des cerises
Et le souvenir que je garde au cœur!

Louise Michel (1830–1905) was a French anarchist, school teacher, medical worker, and important figure in the Paris Commune.[1] She often used the pseudonym Clémence and was also known as the red virgin of Montmartre. Journalist Brian Doherty has called her the "French grande dame of Anarchy."[2] Yale historian John Merriman said: "She embraced the cause of women's rights, proclaiming that one could not separate 'the caste of women from humanity'".[1]

Louise Michel excerpts

"*The Public School! The colleges and other institutions of learning, are they not models of organization, offering the people fine opportunities for instruction? Far from it. The school, more than any other institution, is a veritable barrack, where the human mind is drilled and manipulated into submission to various social and moral spooks, and thus fitted to continue our system of exploitation and oppression.*

"*It is the harmony of organic growth which produces variety of color and form, the complete whole we admire in the flower. Analogously will the organized activity of free human beings, imbued with the spirit of solidarity, result in the perfection of social harmony, which we call Anarchism. In fact, Anarchism alone makes non-authoritarian organization of common interests possible, since it abolishes the existing antagonism between individuals and classes.*

"*Just as the animal cells, by mutual co-operation, express their latent powers in formation of the complete organism, so does the individual, by co-operative effort with other individuals, attain his highest form of development.*

"It therefore logically follows that the greater the number of strong, self-conscious personalities in an organization, the less danger of stagnation, and the more intense its life element.

"Anarchism asserts the possibility of an organization without discipline, fear, or punishment, and without the pressure of poverty: a new social organism which will make an end to the terrible struggle for the means of existence,-- the savage struggle which undermines the finest qualities in man, and ever widens the social abyss. In short, Anarchism strives towards a social organization

Le chant des partisans

Ami, entends-tu le vol noir des corbeaux sur nos plaines?
Ami, entends-tu les cris sourds du pays qu'on enchaîne?
Ohé, partisans, ouvriers et paysans, c'est l'alarme.
Ce soir l'ennemi connaîtra le prix du sang et les larmes.Montez de la mine, descendez des collines, camarades ! Sortez de la paille les fusils, la mitraille, les grenades.
Ohé, les tueurs à la balle et au couteau, tuez vite ! Ohé, saboteur, attention à ton fardeau: dynamite...
C'est nous qui brisons les barreaux des prisons pour nos frères.
La haine à nos trousses et la faim qui nous pousse, la misère. Il y a des pays où les gens au creux des lits font des rêves.
Ici, nous, vois-tu, nous on marche et nous on tue, nous on crève...
Ici chacun sait ce qu'il veut, ce qu'il fait quand il passe. Ami, si tu tombes un ami

> sort de l'ombre à ta place.
> Demain du sang noir sèchera au grand
> soleil sur les routes. Chantez, compagnons,
> dans la nuit la Liberté nousécoute... Ami,
> entends-tu ces cris sourds du pays qu'on
> enchaîne?
> Ami, entends-tu le vol noir des
> corbeaux sur nos plaines ?

Friend, do you hear the black flight of the crows on our plains? Friend, do you hear the deaf cries of the country which one chains? Ohé, partisans, workmen and peasants, it is alarm. This evening the enemy will know the price of blood and tears. Climb out of the mines, come down from the hills, comrades! Get the rifles out of the straw, the grapeshot, the grenades. Ohé, the killers with bullets and knifes, kill quickly! Ohé, saboteur, careful with your burden: dynamite... It is we who break the prison bars for our brothers. Hatred is hunting and hunger pushes us, misery. There are countries where people in beds make dreams.

Here, you see, one marches and one kills and gets killed... Here each one knows what he wants, what he does when he marches. Friend, if you fall a friend will take your place. Tomorrow black blood will dry under the sun on the roads. Sing, companions, in the night Freedom listens to us... Friend, do you hear these deaf cries of the country which one chains? Friend, do you hear the black flight of the crows on our plains?

> Madam' Veto avait promis (bis)
> De faire égorger tout Paris (bis)
> Mais son coup a manqué
> Grâce à nos canonniers.
>
> Dansons la Carmagnole
> Vive le son (bis)
> Dansons la Carmagnole
> Vive le son du canon !

Dansons la Carmagnole
Vive le son (bis)
Dansons la Carmagnole
Vive le son du canon !

Ah ! ça ira, ça ira, ça ira
Les aristocrat's à la lanterne
Ah ! ça ira, ça ira, ça ira
Les aristocrat's on les pendra

Monsieur Veto avait promis (bis)
D'être fidèle à son pays (bis)
Mais il y a manqué,
Ne faisons pas de quartier.

Antoinette avait résolu (bis)
De nous faire tomber sur le cul (bis)
mais son coup a manqué,
Ne faisons pas de quartier.

Amis, restons unis (bis)
Ne craignons pas nos ennemis (bis)
S'ils viennent nous attaquer,
Nous les ferons sauter.

Oui, nous nous souviendrons toujours (bis)
Des sans-culottes des faubourgs (bis)
A leur santé buvons,
Vivent ces francs lurons.

On Vichy, Maréchal Pétain and the hymn see:

http://www.theguardian.com/world/2002/may/11/france.weekend7

About the Author

Claude Beccai is an inveterate storyteller. She has spun yarns since early childhood to spruce up the truth or to give it a twist to capture an audience at odds with reality. As a long time teacher, her gift to arrange facts has served her well with a broad variety of often reluctant students of all ages, background and mixed abilities. Most of her tales have been delivered orally. She has also been involved in live theater where she is known to have belted, off-key, absurd and outrageous lines.

She now lives in Vancouver, Canada where she pursues a complex career of grandmother for two lovely girls, a trekker on well-paved paths and a loiterer at public libraries. She was born quite some time ago and she is not dead yet.

Connect with Claude Beccai

I really appreciate you reading my book! Here are my social media coordinates:

Friend me on Facebook:
http://facebook.com/claudiabeccai

Follow me on Twitter:
http://twitter.com/claudiabeccai

Favorite my Smashwords author page:
https://www.smashwords.com/profile/view/mc

Subscribe to my blog:
http://blog.smashwords.com

Connect on LinkedIn:
http://www.linkedin.com/in/claudiabeccai

Visit my website:
http://www.smashwords.com